PRAISE FOR THE AUTHOR

"Making decisions in life is something that we all do. Either your decisions are empowering you or disempowering you. The question is, which one are you choosing and are you ready to take your decision-making process to another level? Through Steve's unique insights you'll discover new ways of being, having and doing. There isn't anyone else who can articulate an idea and concept like Steve Coleman. Study his principles and your life will never be the same again."

John Spender
Author, Speaker and Coach

"I have had a lifetime of adventures with Steve in the mountains and in the bush, with no disasters. I would go anywhere with him and it is without hesitation that I say, 'Go with Steve in this book.'"

Peter Reimann
Professional Engineer (retired), Current Chairman of a Bush Restoration Group and ongoing Mountain Adventurer

---

"Steve Coleman always maintains a profound balance between logical and intuitive considerations when making decisions, both personally and professionally. Given Steve's balanced approach to 'mindful decision making,' I would highly recommend this valuable resource of 'Decisions, Decisions! How To Make The Right One Every Time.'"

Zoe-Anne Fields
Counsellor and Author, *Transformations*

"I met Steve when participating in a coaching course back in 2011. Steve is an amazing listener with such a calming spirit and he makes you feel so relaxed that a conversation can just flow. With his wealth of knowledge, he is there to guide you through any situation. It is a pleasure to call Steve my friend and I would have no hesitation in recommending his latest book, 'Decisions, Decisions! How To Make The Right One Every Time.'"

Jenny Davison

"Steve is a calm and centred man who has a genuine desire to pursue what creates true happiness. He has inspired me to do the same and will no doubt have the same effect on you. Enjoy the journey and embrace the change."

Amy Proud
Yoga Teacher, Artist, English/Humanities/Religion teacher

"It's a burning question that keeps us awake at night: Am I making the right decision? No one is better equipped to guide you on your decision-making journey than Steve, the Peter Pan of the twenty-first century. Steve brings his youthful optimism, intuition and wisdom to every situation and this book is no different. I know Steve both personally and professionally and I am confident that his methodical approach to decision making will guide you on your life journey and empower you to reach your potential. Steve once told me, "It will *happen." And, of course, it did."*

Katrina Guazzo
B Education, B Journalism, James Cook University, Townsville.
English and Film, Television and News Media Teacher, Ignatius Park College,
Townsville, Australia

"Steve is one of those rare people who are comfortable and balanced with both their emotion/emotive persona and the rational/analytical. He's an amazingly skilled outdoorsman who loves sharing his skills with others, especially young people. But even when teaching/sharing rock-climbing, he is always sharing and role-modelling other things like courage, connectedness, decision-making, commitment and risk management. Steve and I have shared more than 20 years of helping each other with home projects, shifting boulders, lending shoulders, cups of tea and major celebrations. Steve understands that decision-making is always emotional, that indecision is a choice, that making the right decision can sometimes mean making mistakes (if you learn from them) and the importance of going on to make your decisions correct retrospectively, instead of undermining them. I look forward to reading and applying Steve's book in my own decisions in the next few years."

Laurence McCook - Ph.D.
Science-Based Marine Management and Conservation,
Pew Fellow in Marine Conservation,
Adjunct Principal Research Fellow and Partner Investigator, ARC Centre of
Excellence for Coral Reef Studies, James Cook University, Townsville, Australia

"'Decisions, Decisions! How to Make the Right One Every Time' is a wonderful marriage of pragmatism and theory to help a range of people from diverse backgrounds improve the quality of their decision making and, in turn, improve the quality of life for themselves and the significant people in their lives.

In a society where the quality of our relationships is more important than ever before, author Steve Coleman gives us the benefit of his perceptive insight into human behaviour, strong work ethic and unusual sense of humour to give us a tool to make sense of the modern world."

Michael Conn
Principal Ignatius Park College, Townsville, Australia

DECISIONS!
DECISIONS!

GLOBAL
PUBLISHING
G R O U P

Global Publishing Group
Australia • New Zealand • Singapore • America • London

DECISIONS!
DECISIONS!

How to Make the Right One Every Time

STEVE COLEMAN

First Edition 2016

Copyright © 2016 Stephen E Coleman

National Library of Australia
Cataloguing-in-Publication entry:

Creator: Coleman, Steve E. (Stephen Edward), 1950- author.

Decisions, Decisions! How To Make The Right One Every Time / Steve Coleman.

1st ed.
ISBN:9781925288247 (paperback)

Decision making
Success

Dewey Number: 153.83

Cartoons by Heidi Zolker and Timothy Coleman

Published by Global Publishing Group
PO Box 517 Mt Evelyn, Victoria 3796 Australia
Email info@GlobalPublishingGroup.com.au

For further information about orders:
Phone: +61 3 9739 4686 or Fax +61 3 8648 6871

This book is dedicated to Charles Stephen Coleman and Christine Helen Coleman (nee Conrad), my father and mother, who remain two of my greatest champions and decision-makers. They stand with numerous others from whom I have drawn invaluable lessons and inspiration in my life's journey.

The other decision-makers, you will discover listed in the "Acknowledgments" and in references throughout the text of this work.

It is dedicated also to the decision-maker within each one of us, especially within you, the reader. Thus, it is a guide and resource to lighten the load as you take on, one by one, those many courageous decisions ahead of you and, if it carries you only one tiny step forward in your life's mission, then this work has served its purpose.

Stephen E Coleman

ACKNOWLEDGEMENTS

In truth, our achievements are pinnacles. We achieve from the summit of each one, engaging ever more "shoulders" on which to balance with every step we take upwards.

Creating this book is no different and I must thank, with a sense of privilege and deep gratitude, those on whose shoulders I now stand, with completed book in hand.

Darren Stephens and the team at Global Publishing is the living machine that kick-started "Decisions, Decisions" with Spike Hummer on beautiful Hamilton Island in 2010 and who continues to guide, mentor, inspire and help propel this project onwards. Thank you, team, for your uncompromising professionalism and kindness.

Entwined within the messages of this work are the inspiration and special memories of the graduates and leaders of "Coach the Coach" (Gold Coast 2010), Anthony Robbins (UPW 2009 Sydney and DWD Gold Coast 2010), Joel Roberts Enterprise and LOI graduates (Melbourne 2013) and the unstoppable T. Harv Ecker, Quantum Leap team and graduates (Australia, Malaysia and Canada 2012 – 2013).

As always, there are individual movers and shakers who have taught me, encouraged and inspired me. It remains a privilege to have had the opportunity to rub shoulders with such experts, soak up their success mindset and learn from them: Leigh Farnell, (Master of the Acronym) Blue Rocket Business Systems; Pat Mesiti, Millionaire Mindset Club; Jamie McIntyre, 21st Century Academy; Mal Emery, Magnetic Marketing and Publications; Paul Davis, Breakthrough Academy (Thank you Paul for the "clarifiers" in Chapter 10).

To the authors whose books I have found myself going back to over and over and over, thank you for deciding to share your wisdom and insights with such an unflinching intent to make a difference for the better. Of particular mention are Sri Nisargadatta Maharaj, "I Am That"; Deepak Chopra, "Ageless Body, Timeless Mind" and other gems of pure wisdom; Anthony Robbins, "Awaken the Giant Within"; the late Stephen R Covey, "The 7 Habits of Highly Effective People" and Sir Ken Robinson, "The Element."

A special debt of gratitude and thanks is extended to Kathy Kolbe and the "real-deal" team at Kolbe Corp. It was with profound relief that I discovered on reading "Conative Connection," that it was okay for me to do things the way I enjoyed most. Conative profiling, out of the very many agents of change in my life, is an unequivocal, outright winner.

Assembling this work demanded repeated opportunities to "get in the zone," to write, reflect, edit, ponder and edit again. None of these essentials would have been possible without the understanding and trust from my client-colleagues at Ignatius Park College in Townsville, Australia, in particular, Michael Conn, the College Principle, for his unwavering confidence in switching from being my employer to becoming a valued client. Whilst on a "college" note, never has it rung truer that one's students are one's best teachers. I can think of no better time nor place than right now to thank every one of you (over 30 thousand at last approximation), for driving me on to become a better leader, calling me out on cue when I slipped below the bar and for simply being authentically who you are. It's been a blast to have spent time with you, albeit briefly at times.

To those willing stalwarts and true friends who penned the kind words of testimonial on the previous pages and those who took the time to

ACKNOWLEDGEMENTS

respond to the request, I am indebted to you and forever at you service: John Spender, Peter Reimann, Zoe-Anne Fields, Katrina Guazzo, Amy Proud, Laurence McCook, Jenny Davison and Michael Conn. Thank you for your friendship, your trust and your belief in this project.

Zillions of thanks to Heidi Zolker and Timothy Coleman for cleverly embellishing the text's thread of education with your trademark finesse in cartoon lightness. You are true experts of the craft.

Between the peaks of this endeavour, there have been inevitable lows and right "downers" and there is a group of special people who have lovingly borne the brunt of those awkward and sometimes "prickly" vibes which can come with downers. Thank you awesome family! I love you heaps. And to my wife, travelling companion and true friend, Heather, you are one amazing, talented and beautiful lady.

May our own shoulders remain willing and steadfast for those on their own pinnacles of decision-making above us.

CONTENTS

FOREWORD

There is a twentieth century adage which says, "We are what we eat." Permit me to venture a twenty-first century version, "We are the decisions we make."

For better or for worse, conscious decisions are what set us apart from other life forms on the planet. On top of that, inside our mind-space, there is a myriad of unconscious decisions that are made ... those tiny, and often repetitive, changes that slip by us totally unnoticed ... manifestations of change on another, subliminal, level.

The point is that as conscious, aware, thoughtful, enquiring, intellect-rich creatures, making decisions is what we do. It is an integral, inescapable part of every one of us. Deciding is as much a part of us as breathing, eating, drinking, sleeping, sweating, yawning, smiling and so on, and so on, and so on. Making decisions determines our path in life. This way, that way ... the choice is always yours. That's what creates your daily life – moment by moment, decision by decision.

Over the millennia of human history, thinkers, philosophers, scientists, poets and the more recent Bill and Belinda Smiths working their trades, have deployed their wits, engaged superior intellect and well-honed problem-solving skills to make sense of the world. "Have their decisions changed the world? How do the decisions of the other billions of people on this planet affect us and our decisions? And what about the infinity of decisions which are yet to be made to keep the world going or growing. How do they all fit together and make sense?"

Making sense means "making simple."

In this book, *"Decisions, Decisions! How To Make The Right One Every Time,"* you will discover a skilful and succinct "transformation" of this apparent complexity (and sometimes rife, over-whelming confusion) into a simple model for clear decision-making.

It is a user-friendly "translation" of the intricacies of academic language normally used to deal with abstractions such as those of the human mind, into easy, everyday "speak" plus, for your delight, there is a dot-point summary for super-quick uptake of the key messages at the end of each chapter.

What a gift!

The author has artfully drawn in key resonating threads from his introspective experience in consideration of human physiology, biology, demography and spirituality.

Steve's simple model of "right decision-making" engineered within the following pages, is simple and down-to-earth and you may find yourself wondering why a book like this has taken so long to arrive on the international bookshelves.

The E.C.R.O.M.™ Model for making right decisions could very well be the most powerful tool you ever add to your decision-making tool kit.

The especially designed cartoons along the way are a welcome flourish to add further lightness to your reading journey.

Whether you are a grandmother or high school graduate, a theologian or thespian, scientist or single mum and you have been looking for a way to make more empowering decisions, the right decision ...this book is certainly worth a read. It's a gem!

May you make the decisions that create the life and the world you imagine and are excited to live in and be part of. Your decisions do create your future!

Enjoy!

Tracey Stranger
Entrepreneur, Author, Self Mastery Mentor
"How to Overcome Stress Naturally fwd HH The Dalai Lama"
www.HowToOvercomeStressNaturally.com

INTRODUCTION

This book is one of those projects that has been "brewing" a while ... since the early 1970s in fact, when I had just committed to a career in teaching which, in spite of several years training, I didn't feel I really knew much about. I did a reasonable job it would seem, by professional standards, but I constantly carried around a nagging uneasiness that there was something missing ... something not quite right. I was somehow out of alignment or had overlooked something. In those early professional days I believed I wasn't in a position to question much. One did what one had to do to satisfy the "system" of procedures, protocols and what appeared to be mostly positional authority that came with industrial age thinking. (The late Stephen Covey had not yet published his great book, "The Seven Habits of Highly Effective People.")

Uneasiness turned to discontent which turned to frustration. Frustration morphed into exasperation that resulted in a commitment to do something about what wasn't working, whatever that was.

Since then, I'm happy to report, driven by an insatiable curiosity and some rigorous, ongoing and often ruthless introspection, an inevitable reconditioning of my own internal "wiring" provided a new way of looking at the world; in fact, a whole new and different model of the world to the one I had managed to create since drawing my first breath. A new rationality of what I was witnessing around me emerged and with it, a new inspirational direction.

I became aware that people did what they did and thought what they thought in one of two ways:

They either <u>reacted</u>, mostly unconsciously, to their perceptions and let those reactions build their reality and run their lives,

Or they <u>responded</u> knowingly and deliberately to what was going on. They made conscious decisions with the same core toolbox of capabilities that graces every human being on the planet, to create for themselves the world they wanted.

To me, it all boiled down to <u>awareness</u> and <u>choice.</u>

If I could become aware and believe I could create my own future by viewing my past differently, then maybe others could too.

The age-old axiom, "If you want to change the world, you must first change yourself" rang true for me.

Having choices meant making decisions and I realized with a degree of gravity, that my whole life was a bead-string of decisions, one after another, after another, after another.

Everybody made decisions ... all the time ... continuously ... for richer or poorer ... for better or for worse.

That left one critical question remaining: What makes decisions work for people and what makes them not work?

We are constantly bombarded by, and immersed in, a sea of information to which we often have to react very quickly or respond in an informed and intelligent way. If we react, it is mostly without thinking and that can either be helpful (a good habit) or not helpful (a not good habit) depending on our type and level of <u>conditioning</u>.

To respond intelligently requires that we are conscious of that to which we are responding, i.e. the stimulus and also conscious of the processing and actual decision that ensues.

What appears to not to be happening is that people are unable or unwilling to make time for the informed and considered decisions that serve them, i.e. the decisions that are right for them. Neither are they consistently quick enough to strategically intercept their lightning-quick reactions ... the habits that either serve them or disarm them. Instead, they find themselves swept along in a flow of mindless reaction after reaction after reaction with some informed decision in the mix. Consequently, they are often just "keeping their heads above water," "making ends meet," looking after their families, looking after themselves, their health, their finances and making sure their work or business is on track and a myriad of other things that bombard just about every one of us all the time.

The key to breaking free of this mindless, reactive flow is in making right decisions.

A right decision is one that the decision-maker owns. Decision ownership is when the person (or organization) takes full responsibility for it and they accept its outcome no matter what.

This book describes a simple reliable tool to help make those decisions the right ones ... every time. It will guide you through a simple, easy-to-remember process that you can use on yourself or within your organisation at any time and in any place.

When people start to consistently make the right decisions for themselves, an interesting development occurs. What happens, because it's built into a right-decision habit, is that people start to discover that they have talents and capabilities they didn't know they had. These "hidden" talents and capabilities have in fact, always been there. They just haven't had the right environment to manifest into a recognisable form. I concur one hundred percent with Sir Ken Robinson who *"(believes) passionately that we are born with tremendous natural capacities and that we lose touch with many of them as we spend more time in the world. Ironically, one of the main reasons this happens is education. The result is that too many people never connect with their true talents and therefore don't know what they're capable of achieving."*

And so this work is committed to a second and equally important objective: the presentation of a simple, workable structure for individuals and organisations to identify the talents and capabilities with which they are currently working and also to become aware of those they suspected they did have all along but, for whatever reason, are not using to their advantage.

So making right decisions and engaging hidden talents and capabilities go hand in hand. In fact, neither one can exist without the other.

It goes without saying that making more decisions that are right and engaging hidden talents and capabilities, is a sure-fire recipe for improving efficiency and increasing productivity for any individual in their day-to-day life or, for that matter, in any organisation.

Improving efficiency and increasing productivity have been, in one way or another, a prime objective for most human beings since they began walking the planet roughly 2 million years ago. It is not a new phenomenon and there are very many strategies to do this which have been tried and tested over the millennia ... some highly successful, some not so. *"Decisions, Decisions!"* delivers a 21st century version.

If there were two "why's" for creating this work, they would be:

To create a vehicle for quality change and therefore quality learning and growth in the lives of those who choose to step on board the *"Decisions, Decisions"* ship and make a difference

... and to paint a very clear picture of an alternative ... an outside-the-box alternative, free of the subliminal conditioning, and potentially compromising, mentally seductive world of the 21st century in which we could travel if we chose.

The E.C.R.O.M. model for decision-making is that vehicle.

E.C.R.O.M. is our DNA for decision-making ... and as Deoxyribonucleic Acid (DNA) is the blueprint molecule for what makes us who we are physically, E.C.R.O.M. is the blueprint for our every decision where:

E stands for **Event**

C stands for **Critical Space**

R stands for **Reaction** or **Response**

O stands for **Outcome**

M stands for **Measure**

So let's jump in with this brand new acronym and get started right now.

PART I

THE KNOWLEDGE BIT

CHAPTER 1

E - ISOLATING EVENTS

CHAPTER 1

E - IDENTIFY THE EVENT ... PRECISELY

Anything to which we give a meaning is an event. An event only happens because there has been a change to which we have assigned a meaning. No change ... no event ... no meaning.

On the surface, an event is something that happens. For something to happen there has to be a change of some kind, which means there also has to be a witness ... a person to register the change.

Change or event-registering happens in the mind and is represented by activity in particular areas of the physical brain. This happens in a sequence: first there is stimulation via a neutral pathway to parts of the brain, then some processing that requires memory-retrieval and clever neural integration where associations are created and "voila," the event is registered and ready for whatever purpose we have chosen.

Let's take an example. Let's say a bird just pooped on your newly-washed car.

Useful questions to ask are, "When or where did this mental picture of a bird pooping on your car start to take shape? Where or when did this registration process start?"

Without digging into the disciplines of neurology and behavioural sciences, a simple answer would be: When energy of one kind or another strikes one or more of your sensory organs, (eyes, ears, nose, taste buds or skin) and is transformed into a user-friendly signal which travels along a nerve to the brain. Your brain does what it has to do and the process of registration is completed. The stored event is ready for deployment, which could be you deciding to get into a "tizz" because you have to wash your car again or ... you decide it's a sign of good luck because someone once told you about the "bird-poop-good-luck" thing. We will investigate this kind of phenomenon in the next chapter on the Critical Space.

Events of course, are going on all the time ... continuously. We are constantly barraged by incoming energy and it comes in incredible, massive amounts and this poses a very interesting question, "If this energy is coming at us all the time, how come we aren't aware of everything that's happening all the time?"

Well we could, if we choose, close our eyes or put a peg over our nose or put on ear muffs or not eat anything or let our hands get nearly frozen to where our fingers are numb and can't feel anything.

We could easily do all of those things. We could somehow block off all of our senses ... for how long though? Could we stand being in the dark for ever? Would we walk into an oncoming truck or other such massive, mindless, indifferent, terminating hunk? How long could we go without smelling anything or hearing anything or feeling with our fingers and would we really want to die of starvation?

Not a very useful answer you will agree.

The truth, so I'm told, is that we filter out everything that's not relevant at the time and what we decide is relevant varies, depending on our immediate focus.

If you were a counter-intelligence agent, for example, and deciding whether or not to trust the person you are talking to, you would be noticing as much as you possibly could about them and filtering out a lot less than the yogi who is in deep meditation and focusing on "the void" or emptiness and who will be filtering out just about everything because it's not important at the time.

So what we focus on decides which events get registered and which events do not. This is a very important piece of information.

Now all the time this event registration is going on, in the endless sea of event energy, there are some changes that don't get registered straight away, if at all yet they do affect us and are so important that if we did have to consciously process them, we would either be killed rather quickly or suffer inconvenient pain or some catastrophic, physical injury. These are events that potentially threaten our physical wellbeing and even our survival sometimes, for example, when we start to operate in temperatures above or below our safe range of $37.8 - 36.1^{0}C$, when a bug flies too close to our open eyes, when masses of bacteria attack our upper respiratory organs or when our muscles run out of oxygen as we run up a hill. Our brain instantly "grabs" these events and acts on them automatically. It "trims back" the registration part and fast-tracks them using a very, very clever automatic, fast-track system called the autonomic nervous system: Instantly, more of our stored energy is released to cool or warm our body so that our temperature stays in the safe range, our eyes automatically blink to avoid the nasty collision of bug with sensitive eyeball, a cavalry of phagocytes gets deployed to our throat lining to dispatch the invading bacterial intruders; our lungs and heart get a "hurry-up" message to get more oxygen out to our running muscles so we don't "run out of steam" and quit the most beneficial part of the workout. This autonomic system goes on all the time we are alive. It never sleeps. It never rests. There are no shift workers. It goes 24/7 on its own. It keeps us operational and if we choose to look after it, it keeps us in great physical shape too.

"But this is all hands-on and physical. Not all events are like that," you say. "What about when we dream or when we get scared just thinking about something scary?"

These are events too, however, instead of our nose, eyes, taste buds and pain, temperature and pressure receptors in the skin, the brain brilliantly sets up its very own event generator using data and associations that it "borrows" from the store in our memory banks. A kind of internal event loop is created.

For example, when a Post Traumatic Stress Disorder (PTSD) sufferer has an anxiety attack, memories of past trauma do the work of the here-and-now, in-the-flesh "bad guy" event. In this person's mind, the event is recreated to where it triggers a negative anxiety emotion.

Or maybe you've laughed at a joke you just remembered? You didn't need any of your senses to set that up, just a whole lot of internal memory stored in your brain's memory banks.

Probably, the most exciting, the most potentially devastating and the most frustrating internal event loops of them all are the ones we set up for the future ... the wedding next week, the Armageddon prophesy, the deciding goal for a series win or the million-dollar payout. These are loops for events that haven't happened yet and they are exciting, potentially devastating and frustrating because they <u>could</u> happen if we could just do or not do certain things. Therein lies the art and the science of manifesting our dreams, our goals and objectives. (More of this in Part Two)

In between the depression of the PTSD sufferer and your laughing at the joke, there are all of our everyday, internal event loops: our reasons for what we should do and our excuses for why we didn't do them. There are our dreams and our denials, our self-talk and stories and our depressors and our motivators. These are the loops that can flick us out of the saddles of life or get us back up into them to carry on. In the following chapters we will tease all of this out and discover how the **E.C.R.O.M. model of decision-making** is applied to make useful sense of it all. We will find out, for example, what it means when a successful mountaineer says, "When I'm standing on top of the mountain, I know I've summited twice."

For now though, let's dig a little deeper into events and examine what's really going on under the surface. Let's go back to the yogi and ask two more useful questions,

"Why would a yogi or yogini want to focus on nothing and filter out everything?" and, "What advantage or fulfilment would that bring them?"

A yogi or yogini is someone who actively studies the relationship between the physical world he or she experiences and its source. (Yogis include themselves in the physical world.) Any person can become a yogi or yogini. All that's needed is a desire to find out where what's "out there" came from, including themselves, and a commitment to act upon it.

Finding what's between what happens "out there" and where it comes from is a bit like finding out what makes this sentence what it is.

The sentence on this page would not exist without either of two essential ingredients: the printed letters and words and the white paper on which they are printed.

Now, we could write the sentence and have it not appear by making the words white or the paper black. For the time being though, let's stick to the original idea and keep it simple for the sake of clarity.

There is one other subtle component that helps the sentence idea along. Every one of the little black marks on the page means something and every group of those marks means something else. Each, by our definition, is a mini-event collectively making up the sentence which we now know represents a concept or thought or message or idea in our minds.

That's the simple, easy, tangible part. When we are reading, we focus on the letters and words to generate the desired mental events that we put to use as learning or relaxing into a great story or accumulating useful information. The really interesting thing is what we don't focus on i.e. the white paper where the words appear or more specifically, the whiteness or contrasting background needed for the print to appear. With some events now registered in our brain via the meanings we took from the marks on the page, another probing question arises, "What, in our mind, is the equivalent of the white space behind the words ... the "thing" or "stuff" that makes all this reading and comprehension and mental event-juggling possible?" "What is it that provides the contrast for our <u>thoughts</u> to appear?"

"What's the 'stuff' of the space between those thoughts?" What sets up that all-important contrast for them to be recognized?"

May I suggest that this is the "stuff" on which the yogi or yogini so diligently focusses. It is emptiness, void, nothingness; a space of "not thought." Yet, as the essential background or contrasting opposite to our thoughts, it has a purpose and for sure, some awesome potential, because without it there could be no thoughts or ideas, no mental events, no anything.

So why would anyone want to focus on such an elusive "piece" of nothingness?

Because with knowledge, understanding and mastery of this "nothing stuff," we can, with practice, gain control and mastery over our thoughts, our actions and what they collectively create ... and what they create is the exciting, wonderful, tragic, depressing, exhilarating, enigmatic world in which we find ourselves living.

Mastering the space in which our thoughts ride, grants us the power to shape them. It grants us the power to shape and mould our own lives and it grants us the power to create our own ultimate destiny ... and our ultimate destiny is one end of the long, long sequence of events that have created our world ... from our first breath (or even before then), to this present point in time.

Events are the stuff of our lives. We must accept every one of them as important and acknowledge both the visible and invisible backgrounds against which they are presented to us.

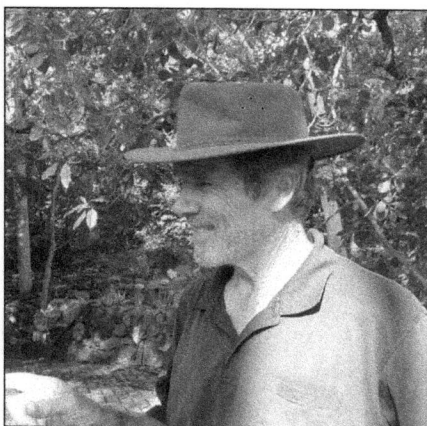

Before we get into the "nitty gritty" of the Critical Space in the next chapter, let's do a short recap of "event" events so far.

CH. 1 FOR THE DOT POINTERS

Identify the event precisely

- An event is something that happens to which we give a meaning.

- Events are registered in your mind when energy comes in to one or more of your sense organs and travels on, via a nerve pathway, to your brain where it is converted into useful information.

- Events are going on all of the time.

- We don't process all of the energy that comes in to our sense organs. Our brains filter out any that are not relevant at the time.

- What you focus on decides what events ultimately get registered in your mind.

- Not all events registered in your mind depend on your sense organs.

- The brain can create its own events by borrowing data and associations from your memory banks and setting up <u>event loops</u>.

- Event loops for the future are essential in your planning and can create positive and negative emotions associated with what <u>could</u> happen.

- Everyday event loops create our reasons for doing and not doing, our excuses and our self-talk, our ideas and inspirations and our depressors and motivators.

- There are two essential parts to every event: the signal or sign or symbol to which we have an assigned meaning and a contrasting background that makes it perceivable e.g. the white background makes the black words appear on the white page as a sentence.

- For your thoughts to become recognizable they must similarly rest on an equivalent contrasting background. There is an intangible and necessary space between your thoughts.

- Being aware of the space between your thoughts helps you control and master them.

SOME FOOD FOR THOUGHT

What happens to all the incoming energy you filter out before it reaches your brain? Do the changes represented by that filtered-out energy really happen?

C

CHAPTER 2

C - KNOW YOUR CRITICAL SPACE

CHAPTER 2

C - YOUR CRITICAL SPACE IS THE CRUCIBLE OF YOUR WORLD - GET TO KNOW IT INTIMATELY

Your Critical Space is where meaning is forged from the reality of that which is, into the illusory substance of time and space thereby creating the most elusive fabrications of all ... the mischievous trickeries of past, present and future.

Your Critical Space is that "zone" between an event happening in your life and the action you take (or don't take) as a result.

In other words, it is the "space" between incoming energy that stimulates your brain and the activity which that stimulation generates in your inner and outer worlds.

Your Critical Space is the workshop of machinery and materials of your mind. Some of those machines and materials you were born with and some you have collected along the way, deliberately or otherwise.

It is also your mind's dressing room of mirrors and make-up and its wardrobe of preferences, idiosyncrasies and rules. It grooms and manicures and readies events in the space for specific and pre-determined actions that you are about to take (or not take).

In addition, your Critical Space is your spiritual foundry where your own pure uniqueness is cast into the many personalities of your current lifetime, the personalities you've already been and the ones you have yet to become.

Your Critical Space is itself a tool. It is a mind tool designed specifically to explain the transformation from whatever it is that stimulates you into the actions you take as a result.

So, what's in this Critical Space, this workshop or dressing-room of the mind?

As in any work space, there are materials ... the "stuff" that's used to make something or the "stuff" we work on to repair or upgrade. In your Critical Space the materials are the registered events that have arrived either through your senses or from the internal loops your mind sets up from its memory store of facts and figures. Something that's really useful to know is that some of the facts and figures in your memory banks are stored in <u>wrapping</u> and when they are remembered, the wrapping comes too. Those wrappings are feelings.

For example, the green and white runners you were wearing when a brown snake shot across your foot and scared the living daylights out of you as you power-walked along that river track years ago or the Billy Joel number that was playing in the background when you had your first romantic kiss. The fear and anxiety of a possible and untimely end to your life comes whenever you put on your green and white shoes or even just when you think about them as does the feeling of rapturous kiss bliss every time you hear Billy's number one again ... and again ... and again.

The event and the emotion are tied together, sometimes very tightly, in your memory store.

Events like these, the snakes and the kisses, are easy to remember. They can pop up and intrude upon or enhance your mental train without notice. They are close to the surface because they have strong emotional wrappings. The strong emotion makes them easier to remember.

What about the event memories that don't come up, especially when they are urgently needed ... when you need the information instantly ... right now.

"Where did I leave my car keys? I'm sure I left them on the fridge when I came in and I really must go ... now!"

Or the address where you had to pick up your new business partner?

Or the dimensions of the new desk you want to buy and that you have to carry home in your tiny car?

That crucial information is there. You know it's there and you engage all manner of forensic, mental contortions to trigger its release. You rack your brains in abject frustration. All you want to do is reinstate the certainty you had before and get on with whatever it was you were doing.

The keys eventually do turn up. The address is remembered in the nick of time and the dimensions did come to mind, all after a little mental "digging around," "back-tracking" and helpful, learned self-talk you practised for such occasions.

The whereabouts of the keys, the address and the dimensions of the desk were in fact locked away in a big room that adjoins your Critical Space called your <u>subconscious</u>. It's where all the "stuff" goes that you can't remember. It's also where some of the "big stuff" goes that you don't want to remember, like the fall over the balcony when you were five or the rush to hospital with a bloody and painful broken leg after the bike accident or the pain of the Post Traumatic Stress Disorder sufferer. In fact, most of your whole past life lives there. Your subconscious is so spacious, looking into it through its one and only door. It is a bit like looking in through the door of Dr. Who's Tardis. If you are not a Dr. Who person, this simply means the inside is enormously more spacious than the outside would suggest. ("Dr Who" is a BBC science fiction television series created in 1963 and is still running today.)

The good news is that the door between your Critical Space and your subconscious is open all the time. If it wasn't, there's no way you would have found your keys or remembered your new business partner's address or how big the desk was.

So your Critical Space contains some everyday, conscious, mental work-space, some conscious event material with an ever-open doorway into an incredibly, unbelievably massive, memory store of events and of facts and figures and attached emotions.

Now it's at this point in our Critical Space exploration where things start to get interesting.

If this was all that happened in our Critical Space, life would be quite simple and probably a tad boring because all we would do is experience, remember (or forget) and do.

As well as the workspace and materials and the adjoining room of subconscious phenomena, there are several other intangible parts. In a workshop, there are tools and machines for working with wood and there are others for different kinds of metal. The dressing room has manicuring apparatus and procedures suitable only for finger and toe nails and the systems and protocols and equipment specific for hair care. In our minds, there are different types of **processors** that work with mental energy, including registered event energy, each in their own specific way.

These processors are high-level, critical processing systems of your mind-space that keep all the activity in the mental work-space ordered, directed and useful to you ... mostly. There are five of them. Each one fine-tuned, each one different and each one working in sync with each of the others all of the time ... well, hopefully all of the time.

They are: Your **Chunks and Bits** processor (cognitive), your **Feelings** processor (affective), your **I-Will Energy** processor (conative), your **Physical Energy** processor (psychomotor) and your **Me Energy** processor (spiritual).

Sometimes, just as the newly reconditioned motor you happen to be working on runs rough because the timing is still a tad out or the dressing-room hairdryer is performing oddly because you-know-who used it to fast-track a paint job on the same car, there are mental blocks and glitches that dither and stress us from time to time because our mental processors are out of sync with each other. Some are mild inconveniences and we ride over them while others are outright disastrous, awful stretches of mental turmoil that can ruthlessly drag us down and potentially destroy us.

In order to get the very best from the next few chapters, it's worth now taking a closer look at each of these mental processing systems in turn.

Before we do, please remember that the idea of a mental processor is just that. It is an idea ... a mental construct invented purely to assist in explaining and understanding something we can't see or hear or smell or taste or touch like electricity or gravity, radio waves or magnetism.

Having said that, it is important to keep in mind that each of these mental energy processing systems has a physical counterpart in our physical brain. Evidence of their activity in specific parts of the brain shows up consistently with the use of modern scanning machines such as electroencephalograms or EEGs.

It's timely to pause and recap on our exploration of the Critical Space so far ... just to make sure, right now, that your mental energy processors are as much in sync as possible. If you are a dot-point person, you will appreciate this.

CH. 2 FOR THE DOT POINTERS

Your Critical Space is the Crucible of Your World. Get to Know it Intimately.

- **Your Critical Space is the mental space between an event happening in your life and the action you take or don't take as a result.**

- **Your Critical Space works with registered events that have arrived either through your five senses or via internal loops your mind sets up itself from its store of memories.**

- **Most memories are recalled with feelings attached. Strong attached feelings often make remembering easier.**

- **Your subconscious stores what you can't recall and memories too traumatic to easily remember.**

- **In your Critical Space are different mental energy processors that keep your mental energy operations orderly, directed and useful to you.**

- **Your five mental energy processors are: Your Chunks and Bits processor, your Feelings processor, your Physical Energy processor, your I-Will (do this) processor and your Me Energy processor.**

- **The idea of a mental energy processing system or mental energy processor, is a mental construct or aid created purely to assist in explaining and understanding something we can't experience with our senses.**

- **Mental energy processors have identifiable counterparts in your physical brain.**

- **When studied scientifically, the terms used to describe these mental processors approximate to cognitive (Chunks and Bits processor), affective (Feelings processor), psychomotor (Physical Energy processor), conative (I-Will processor) and spiritual (Me processor).**

2.1 YOUR CHUNKS AND BITS MENTAL ENERGY PROCESSOR.

This processor works with the mental energy of certainty, logic and reason. It manipulates and manoeuvres the mental energy of, "I-need-to-do-this-<u>because</u> "

Your certainty or logic processor only works in clear, defined chunks and bits of information. (A bit is the smallest piece of information in a decision that has a meaning, e.g. a letter "a." A chunk consists of a number of "bits" strung together and which has a meaning also, e.g. the word "ask.")

Your Chunks-and-Bits processor is your mental processor of all that is certain.

If anything uncertain "rocks up" at this processor's "door", it won't get a hearing until it is either given a meaning or it is put in a big bag labelled "<u>Uncertainty.</u>" Attached to that "Uncertainty" bag will also be an assortment of other tags like "Possible Explanations Why," "Hypotheses" or "For Further Investigation" or "Needs Some Rigorous Examination and Testing."

If you know science or are a mathematician reading this, you will recognize the signs of "Empirical Science," "The Scientific Method" or the mathematical rigors of logic and deduction.

This certainty-processing system is not all science and maths and logic however. Processing chunks and bits of chopped-up, well-defined, measured-out information happens in just about anything you could think of doing. In our mechanical workshop, for example, making final adjustments to the engine timing to get that exquisite, melodic, satisfying "purr," when the motor runs to its sweet mechanical perfection, demands definite and precise knowledge of motor parts and how they work together. Additionally, figuring out how to get that sweet sound is absolutely essential. What's the procedure, the order of steps that must be followed and what other engine components should be checked before the next step in the tuning sequence is attempted?

If you were writing an assignment for your final acting qualification, the same sequenced and informed steps of logic apply. The assignment must be ordered. It must have the certainty of known facts and of tried and tested ideas. The uncertainties and unknowns and hypotheses, which are also necessary for a convincing delivery, must be addressed using learned rules and acceptable procedures of debate and discussion.

What's worth noting at this point, since we are talking about assignments, is that this processing system of logic, reason, intellect and justification has been the main driver for the past three centuries of mainstream, western education. It has been, and mostly still is, an education driven by relying upon, and largely championing, our human cognitive ability. It is an education system that has demanded measurement across the great continuum of human endeavour ... of how well we use our energy of certainty ... how good (or bad) we are at cognition and how sharp our intellect is.

Numbers have even been assigned to unit changes in our level of performance. This is our I.Q. or <u>Intelligence Quotient</u>.

Our certainty processor ... our logic, particle-and-measurement-infused juggler of chunks and pieces of information, is therefore that which provides the whole framework on which we have structured our modern thinking. It is a sounding board too, if you like, for new ideas or reference points for editing and maybe "turfing out" old ones.

It is a vital part of our critical space. It is not however, the only part and it may well not be the most important one either.

Time for a short recap.

CH. 2.1 FOR THE DOT POINTERS

Your Chunks and Bits Energy Processor

- **Your Chunks and Bits processor works with the mental energy of certainty, logic and reason. It works with identifiable pieces (chunks and bits) of information.**

- **Uncertainty is handled by your Chunks and Bits processor via asking questions and assigning labels to uncertainty like "possible explanations," "hypotheses," "for further investigation" and "requires rigorous examination and testing."**

- **The Chunks and Bits mode of mental processing has been the main driver of mainstream western education for at least the past three centuries.**

- **I.Q. or Intelligence Quotient is one measure of how we perform logically.**

- **Your Chunks and Bits processor is not the only part of your Critical Space nor is it necessarily the most important.**

2.2 YOUR FEELINGS ENERGY PROCESSOR

Your Feelings Energy processor is your mental system for processing emotional energy. It is sometimes called your affective system and it's out there on its own when it comes to uniqueness because just about whatever our chunks and bits (or cognitive) energy processor is, our feelings processor is not.

That means there are no chunks and bits of packaged energy. No defined, identifiable, measurable pieces of information ... and not much packaged certainty, if any at all.

What characterises your emotional energy processor most of all is its ability to easily influence, and sometimes even take control of your actions, your physical appearance and most important of all, the way you make decisions.

In the course of likely human evolution, emotion has had a very, very, very, very important role because over and over and over and over and over again, it has kept us from annihilation ... from being wiped off the map, from being eaten by sharks or dying of snake bite. The one feeling ... the one emotion that works this life-preserving magic and keeps us breathing and enjoying life above ground is the emotion of being afraid, i.e. the emotion of <u>fear</u>.

Fear is probably the most potent and the most powerful "brew" of raw emotional energy our brains will ever have to process.

"So how could one single feeling be so important and do all of that?"

It does all of that because fear is a red flag. It is the red flag of danger, the red flag of caution. It is the "watch-out" flag.

"If you take one step further, things could get very, very sticky for you."

"Do not go there!"

"Danger!"

"Back off!"

"Run like the proverbial!"

Your emotional energy processing system raises that flag the instant it retrieves a memory of one of those past events from your mental store, gift-wrapped in emotion by the very occasion when it was forged ... in pain or trauma; terror or heart wrenching sadness. For example, the unbearable, withering sting in your toddler hand when you reached up to the hot BBQ plate you thought was just another funny table or when a shark really did brush your leg while you waited beyond the breakers in the cold for the next perfect wave or the palpitating "close shave" when your car suddenly spun out of control on an icy road when driving home from a winter time "grave-yard shift" at work.

Without a well-oiled, ever-ready, in-sync emotional energy processing system, we simply would not survive. We need it desperately ... every day ... all the time!

All however, is not pain and fear and trauma. There are emotional energies that are sweet and sublime and beautiful. There is love and compassion, happiness and satisfaction and many more energies. These energies also work for us however, in a different way. In the capable circuitry of our Feelings processor, they fuel us for the journey. They charge us and motivate us to emotional heights sublime ... unbelievable states where we easily move every one of the proverbial mountains before us.

Whether experiencing pain or pleasure, trauma or titillation, our Feelings Energy processor provides us with the fuel to "run the race." It monitors and adjusts and records that fuel supply ... and it is still there at the end, already fuelling your down-time and recuperation or pouring in to prepare for your next exciting episode of life.

Your emotion-processing system, as we have seen, is not a one-stop shop. It needs help and shortly we will explore some combinations. What do we experience, for example, when Chunks and Bits processing works hand-in-hand with our Feelings processor. What actually happens in your world that you could recognize when an interaction like this happens?

Before we answer the question, we need to recap on our Feelings processor.

CH 2.2 FOR THE DOT POINTERS

Your Feelings Energy Processor

- **Your Feelings energy processor is your mental system for processing emotional energy.**

- **Emotional energy is characterized by its ability to easily influence and sometimes take control of your actions, your physical appearance and your capacity to make decisions.**

- **The emotion of fear helps keep us alive because it fuels our flight away from pain and suffering.**

- **Fear is the red flag of DANGER.**

- **Memories of past events are recalled from our memory banks wrapped in the emotion of the occasion in which they were formed.**

- **As well as "escape" emotions of fear, there are pleasurable emotions like love, compassion, happiness and satisfaction.**

- **All emotions fuel us for the journey, either away from the pain and suffering of something that's hurting us or towards the pleasure of reaching our objectives and goals.**

- **Your Feelings processor monitors and adjusts your emotional fuel delivery with help from your other mental energy processors.**

- **Emotional energy is also delivered for down time, recuperation and preparation for the next decision to be made.**

2.3 YOUR PHYSICAL ENERGY PROCESSOR

Your physical energy processor is everything to do with organizing and deploying your physical energy, e.g. your energy of metabolism (staying alive) and physical movement. It includes the energy needed to keep your heart pumping and the energy you need to walk up stairs or ride a bike or even to sleep. You don't notice some of this energy deployment because it is a subliminal or unconscious experience. The energy is moved around and stored up and taken away without you ever noticing. You don't have to make decisions about how fast your heart has to pump to shift blood. Deciding whether or not to slow it down or speed it up is not required. Your heart beats and beats and beats for the span of your earthly life, alongside other vital organs like your lungs and liver, your bladder and your brain. They too get their jobs done effectively, silently and automatically.

So, what happens when they don't get all the energy they need?

Answer: Very catastrophic times are very close to the door and it will be sent spinning off its hinges unless something changes very, very quickly.

This kind of physical energy supply is vital!

If the supply rate drops below a critical threshold, your chances of losing it all and leaving this beautiful, physical earth for ever are seriously increased.

Survivors of horrific situations ... of dehydration, hunger or hypothermia will attest to that. The humble connoisseur even, of simple, healthy eating and fitness is witness to just how sensitive we are to energy depletion in this quietly efficient and crucial energy-processing system.

Outside of this unconscious automation, the story is a bit different. In your non-automated mental precinct, you are quite conscious of your of energy consumption. You are aware, for example, of how much you use.

You can choose to conserve it or to use it, depending on what you are doing ... even using it more efficiently to get where you want to go can be a choice.

We have only to consider the experts ... the committed athletes, the professional dancers, any people for that matter, who are interested in their personal health and well-being.

Every one of these fitness-conscious, health-and-well-being seekers understands the connection between their exertion levels and their energy supply.

This physical energy processing system, or psychomotor system as it is referred to in science, and educational psychology (Benjamin Bloom 1913 – 1999), is the focus and life-blood of sports coaches, trainers, teachers, physiotherapists and health practitioners across the globe. Their development and nurturing of "well-oiled," efficient, fine-tuned psycho-motor systems, in sync with compatriot cognitive and emotional processors, has given the world over and over and over the great champions: Sir Donald Bradman, Dame Margot Fonteyn, Tiger Woods, Greg Norman and Dame Joan Sutherland. The list goes on and it is endless. It is endless because wherever there is human endeavour, there are champions.

Every one of these iconic achievers has seized upon their own unique set of talents, stalked and studied the experts and honed their physical energy processors to superlative and exceptional effect.

The great news is that it's not the stars only who can reach these dizzy pinnacles of achievement, **every human being on the planet has a gift, within which is the seed and potential that can**

carry them steadfastly and surely to sublime heights of achievement and unquestionable, satisfying success.

All that they (and you and I) need, is to <u>commit</u> to finding that talent ... to commit to discovering that unique and special gift within, that exclusive and often hidden talent that we each have and that no other person on the planet can claim from us. All it's waiting for is that internal "clarion signal" that says, "Start looking now! And don't look back."

Now the distilled version for the Dot Pointers

CH 2.3 FOR THE DOT POINTERS

Your Physical Energy Processor

- **Your Physical Energy processor is everything to do with organizing and deploying your physical energy.**

- **It works with the energy of movement and regulation, both at the cellular level and at that of your physical, body behaviour.**

- **Your physical energy is the energy of your body temperature, movement, heartbeat, sleeping and countless other physical activities you carry out consciously and unconsciously.**

- **When your vital organs don't get all the energy they need, your chances of remaining healthy and alive are reduced. A stroke and a cardiac arrest are examples.**

- **In your conscious, or non-automatic mental space, you can choose to conserve or use up you physical energy.**

- **Your physical energy processing system approximates to the psycho-motor system referred to in science and educational psychology. (Ref. Benjamin Bloom 1913 – 1999)**

- **Practitioners in the sports, wellness and health industries focus primarily on the physical energy processing system.**

- **Your Physical Energy processor is that part of your mental space that tends and supports and maintains your physical presence throughout the highs and lows of your life's journey.**

2.4 YOUR I WILL (DO THIS) ENERGY PROCESSOR

That "clarion signal" from the previous section is the sound and smoke of your mind's discharging starter-gun. The trigger is pulled and the sound and smoke launch you full tilt into the imminent race. It has delivered the mental "go" signal for your race ... the race to which you put up your hand and said, "Yes. It's time to do." (You may not necessarily remember that bit). That same sound and smoke has given the "Go" signal of every race you have run in your life and it will signal the start of every race that remains, whether it's the pursuit of your dream now that you know what you're good at, a full-on, adrenalin-pumping escape from a foraging shark, a slow, methodical game of chess or a simple walk on the beach.

The energy of this "neuro-sounding" gun is that energy which sets you in motion to do something and it is the energy that drives you onwards to the finish line. It is the energy of silent and committed focus and it will be there with you even when the race is done, to refill your tanks of intent and drive and determination and to ready you for the next stretch of your life's road ahead.

This "I-Will" energy is pretty much your energy of conation or your conative energy. **Conative energy is survival, instinctual energy. Without it, we would have the surrender flag up and we would quit at the slightest barrier.** With our conative energy processor in full swing however, we stay the course and persevere until we are satisfied. Many a great survival story is told where this king of energy processing has won the day ... from death zone mountaineers to round-the-world yachtsmen and women. When caught between the proverbial "rock and a hard place," in every instance, every survivor has been driven and whipped and cajoled to press on with this brand of mental energy, to never give up, to "hang in there" no matter what and then to rest and recover and heal.

Unlike our processors of Cognitive, Emotional, Me and Physical energy, your I-Will processor has a rather subtle peculiarity. Not only does this conative system provide the energy of drive and will for you to run your races, it also provides you with a unique set of tracks on which to run them. The really interesting and not widely known news is that every one of us has our own unique set of tracks. In her break-through book, "_The Conative Connection,_" Kathy Kolbe clearly outlines evidence that we have our very own, hard-wired method for how we best do whatever it is we do. If we are left to our own devices, we will very likely do it this way because it works best for us.

You would have to agree it so, so nice to do things "your" way.

When we are given the freedom (and encouragement) to operate in this way, the world suddenly becomes a much more exciting and motivating place.

It can be a different story though, when people are set up <u>against</u> their natural/instinctive way of getting things done. For example, in a team-building exercise, where a group has been given a simple task to accomplish together, some people will do it this way, some that way and some, another "wacky" way.

Sometimes the task is completed smoothly, sometimes not and sometimes not much happens at all. The group becomes a melting pot of directed, and sometimes misdirected, energy, of chunks and bits energy, feeling, physical and spiritual energy all working together to get a result or not working together and not getting a result. We will explore that in more detail later in Part II of this book. We will also explore the really, really interesting question, "What would it be like to do things the way you're wired to, all the time?"

Your I-Will processor is your very own reference point for your uniqueness in the world. It provides you with a mental measuring tool to spot where you differ from those with whom you work and live and play.

Your I-Will dot point summary coming right up.

CH 2.4 FOR THE DOT POINTERS

Your I-Will Energy Processor

- **Your I-Will (Do this) Energy is the energy which determines how you will <u>do</u> (something). It is also the energy of committed focus that drives you onwards to complete a task.**

- **I-Will energy is the same as energy of <u>conation</u> or conative energy.**

- **Unlike your processors of Chunks and Bits, Feelings, Me and Physical energy, your I-Will processor also provides you with a personal, wired-in method for how to best do what you have to do.**

- **Your I-Will processor is your own reference point for your uniqueness amongst those people with whom you work and live and play.**

2.5 YOUR ME ENERGY PROCESSOR

Your Me Energy processor could be regarded as an apparently elusive bit of your inner space. It's an inseparable "thread" in every one of us and the "thread" that holds just about all of what we do together. It is <u>apparently</u> elusive because it is so "big" and "obvious" that it's pretty much invisible most of the time however, it is there.

Your "Me" energy is your "You-ness" energy.

Let's take a more practical example to help explain.

If you were a specialist in making wooden doorways, you would have a set of plans for each different kind of doorway that you had to make. If you were a costume or hat or shoe maker, same deal, you would use the same plan or blueprint or template every time you wanted to make a particular item.

In nature, the exact same strategy applies. In this way, nature gives us birds, wasps, sharks, rock crystals, snowflakes, viruses, mushrooms and yes, human beings as well. **Our Me Energy system is our blueprint for everything human ... teeth and toe nails, breasts and brains, derrieres and DNA.**

We each have a unique Me Energy system. That means it makes me, me, you, you and us, us and it leaves a trail of evidence all around that's so very easy to find should we care to look.

For example, whenever we get a scratch or cut or even a traumatic gaping, gashy, gushing wound, our Me Energy is there on the job immediately immediately ... because it's always been there. The "scratchy" or "gushing" incident scene is flooded with all manner of front-line first-aiders, paramedics ... biochemical, miracle-making bits of us, streaming to obey the human template with its Me Energy system procedures and rules.

Soon the blood stops oozing or squirting away and eventually the muscles and skin start joining back together and the breach closes, first with a sticky, "bogging-up" goo, then some crusty sealant goo followed by an eventual smooth patch of skin with nothing much to show other than a signature scar with its own unique emotional label stored away in our memory for when our other processors need it.

There are other instances where Mother Nature shows us the artistry of her trump card in blueprint "Me" magic. In many tropical and sub-tropical regions of the world are small, innocuous reptiles that really should be living under the bark of trees and flakes of rock or amongst the leaves and branches of far-away jungles, or just outside in our back yard will do.

You wish!

Instead, they seem to prefer the convenience of cavities and crannies of our bedrooms and kitchens and ceilings, computers, TVs and toasters ... wherever there's a scrap of cover or a place to hide. You may have caught one of these harmless little creatures and held it gently by its tail with its body resting on the palm of your hand when a quite unexpected and amazing thing happens. To your utter astonishment, the creature skitters from your hand and effortlessly escapes the intrusion to the nearest dark corner or convenient haven of inaccessibility. Between your thumb and forefinger, you are left with a writhing, wriggling, wormy "thing" ... a gecko tail!

... and there's no blood, no tatters of flesh, no stump of bone ... just a strange solitary wriggly end ... a solitary "un-live" gecko tail. The story doesn't end there. In a month or so, you see on the wall above the night light in the bathroom, that same escapee critter. To your utter amazement, it is sporting a brand spanking new and perfect terminal appendage. It has grown a new tail. The gecko-energy template has done its work impeccably. That once divided gecko is again whole and displaying its unique "gecko-ness". (Did the tail grow a new gecko? No, it didn't.)

Plants can do the same replacement "trick" yet in a much more subtle way.

Or on a more familiar note, a human amputee may be missing an arm or a leg or finger or toe however, chances are, that amputee will report at some time or another, sensing that their arm or leg or finger or toe is still there ... attached, yet not attached ... a ghost appendage.

While we may not be able to grow back a lost limb or severed digit right now, medical scientists and researchers are certainly working on it.

We can however, rest assured, with unquestionable confidence, that our Me Energy processing system is there for us, upholding the template laws and rules for our repair and for our growth ... that magical transformation from those first two cells of conception to a most incredible, wonderful, amazing human "me" and human "you."

Let's dig a little deeper beneath this human template, Me Energy processing idea.

It's one thing to have a "bomb-proof," indestructible plan to keep us unique and human, another to be aware of it and yet another to fully appreciate and accommodate its unbelievable power and significance.

Not only does our Me Energy processor keep us what we are physically, it also provides us with an invisible, multi-storied "tower' from which to view and interact with the world, and yes, it also grants us wilful access to any of the viewing levels whenever we choose.

Let's take an example. Let us return to our friendly, occasionally microwave-destroying gecko for a moment ... the one with the new tail.

That gecko has got to eat and to eat, it has to stalk and creep and steal and pounce to secure the moth or mosquito (or straw with which you may be teasing it).

Now we can't be exactly sure, yet probably that gecko doesn't think too much about the whole affair of getting the food. Its "gecko-ness" somehow seems to take care of all that; its arrival at the "food-getting" place on the wall above the night light, the stalking, the catching and the eating, just happen. The gecko just does gecko "stuff."

Most human beings have much more going on for them at meal times; there is a consciousness and awareness factor. We know that we are eating. We are aware there are some serious and complicated energy transfers going on from when we first get to feel or touch or smell or taste the food, to when bits of it come out, somewhat transformed, at the back end. We might also offer a blessing for its arrival and its presence before us and then maybe offer a thank you to whatever or whomever we believe is responsible for its timely delivery.

Our Me Energy processor looks after this kind of rite and ritual and very many other acts like it all the time ... and there's a neat spin-off: we get set up with a way to seriously and easily handle the big question ... the big question that's driven some thinkers to destruction and some great nations forever apart ... the question of "Life, The Universe and Everything." (Douglas Adams 1982)

In a way, your Me Energy system is also your "Being" template. It's the plan you have to simply be ... the plan or blueprint that allows you to experience the world and yourself on different levels, that is, from different storeys of your personal "humanness" viewing tower.

If you choose to read on, you may see how the outside world and the inner one that you hold secure and sometimes secret, are simply different views from that exact same Me Energy "skyscraper." Your awareness vantage point or Me Energy viewing platform changes.

What hasn't and doesn't change when we switch storeys or platforms, is that from which our Me Energy comes ... the point source from which your Me Energy and all of your other energies and systems and processors come ... the pure singularity of creation ... the Ultimate Source, God or any other equivalent you have chosen as your reference centre and guiding light.

In the "deck" of human energy playing cards, Me Energy is your "trump suit." These dot points are crucial.

CH 2.5 FOR THE DOT POINTERS

Your Me Energy Processor

- **Your Me Energy Processor (Spiritual) maintains the energy template that keeps you human and allows you to shift your awareness between different Me Energy levels and experience yourself and the world in different ways.**

- **The Me Energy equivalent in a gecko is the energy that grows the gecko a new tail when it loses it accidently or sheds it to escape from being caught.**

- **Human amputees sometimes report feeling a ghost limb where their removed appendage used to be.**

- **Your Me Energy processing system repairs and directs healing using your human template or blueprint to restore your unique "you-ness" after you have been physically damaged.**

- **Rites, rituals and reflections that relate to your reason for being (on the planet) are fueled by your Me Energy.**

- **Although your mental viewing point of the world may change, the source of your "being" energy is constant.**

R

CHAPTER 3

R - REACTION OR RESPONSE?

CHAPTER 3

R - "AM I RESPONDING OR REACTING?" ASK YOURSELF THIS QUESTION ... CONSTANTLY.

It doesn't matter whether you respond or you react. What matters is that you do so with Commitment, Passion and above all, Ownership.

So, now we come to the third and crucial part of the E.C.R.O.M. decision process ... the "R" part ... the "Reaction or Response" piece of the "equation" ... or depending on what's going on in your Critical Space, the "Reaction <u>and</u> Response" part.

Remember that your Critical Space is where registered events (from your sense organs or internal thought loops) are received and nurtured and moved around by your five great mental energy processors.

These key mental systems, you will recall, are: Your Chunks and Bits Processor (Cognitive), your Feelings Processor (Affective), your I-Will Processor (Conative), your Physical Energy Processor (Psychomotor) and your Me Energy Processor (Spiritual).

As a serious decision-maker yourself, you may well ask, "Well, what comes next? What happens now that all of this streamlined, engineered, amazing, orchestrated, mental "buzz-buzz" has happened in my Critical Space?"

What comes next is a brand new, never-seen-before piece of you in action ... or sometimes not in action.

This action (or not action) may be a raging, frothing, tyrannical, impossibly awful, miserable, destructive "hissy fit" of the highest magnitude or it could be the sweet song in your mind's eye on your first 4,000 metre summit or maybe nothing at all ... a fizzer ... a neutral "ho-hum" ... "zilch-worth" of inaction, like after watching a rather "flat" movie.

Action or no action ... sweet singing or sour grapes, you either <u>reacted</u> to that recently registered and processed event or you consciously <u>responded</u> to it.

Your Critical Space has done its work with due diligence, drawn up a plan of action, set the appropriate measures of emotional energy to fuel what's coming next, engaged and coordinated your five mental processors and applied the rules, the protocols and the procedures that they determined were right for the registered event in the pipeline. Now it's over to your physical body to do its thing ... to carry out the instructions in that Critical Space package ... to throw that gushing hopeless tantrum, to sweetly sing on the mountain top or to scratch your right ear after a bee just flew close to it. Maybe it's to take a "rain check" and leave the action for another time or even pass it completely ... do nothing at all. Your physical body can and will do all of those things once it gets the signal from your I-Will processor "starting gun."

Now, does your Critical Space ever drop off to sleep? Does it wash its hands of the embarrassing tantrum? Does it "leave you in the lurch" on the summit when the nearby cornice suddenly breaks off without warning?

Absolutely not! Your Critical Space is still whirring and humming industriously away like a workshop or buzzing and babbling like an energised dressing room ... still loyally with you ... an eye in the sky, yet still attached and monitoring your every move, your every thought, your every nuance of body language, your every energy state. It's like a veteran puppeteer, poised and watching his beloved puppets from above, ready to make the next piece of the story happen and flow on to the next and the next and the next.

An example will put all this into more practical terms.

Let's say you are feeling hungry.

You could feel hungry for a whole lot of reasons. For the time being though, let's keep the scenario simple. Let's say you've just got back home from a 10 kilometre jog ... your three-times-a-week nature fix and workout with a friend (who's already gone home). Your energy reserves are a little down and need a top up.

A useful question to ask right now is, "Where did this hungry feeling actually start? What event must your Critical Space have registered to make you "do hungry?"

The registered event started out very, very small, unnoticed and unconscious. Some cells in your body, including some leg muscle cells ... had used their energy supplies up and sent out a neurological signal for some more to your central nervous system (your spinal cord and brain). This is a mini-biochemical event that was propelled, at incredible speed, into your Critical Space for immediate registration as the main event i.e. consciously feeling hungry. A neuro impulse was given a meaning. Registration was immediate because doing nothing about this shortage could seriously compromise your core energy reserves.

Your Feelings Processor smartly retrieved some emotionally wrapped "hungry" memories to work on i.e. the lingering memory of the sweetness of a towering chocolate cake wedge at the end of the winter bike ride last year. There's the nauseous, "poor-me" wretchedness of the food poisoning episode on a mountain trek not so long ago and there's the wonderful, vital feeling of the cool freshness of a fruit smoothie you made for yourself and your running partner after an exhilarating workout on the track last week. The question is, "Which of these competing memories will direct the action you are about to take?"

Your Physical Processor has already "put in some yards" too, receiving the incoming "top up" signals and is working hard on setting you up to physically go where the food is and eat. It's only waiting for the go-ahead from your **I-Will Processor** which has, by now, charted a course for how you need to prepare and eat your food for maximum satisfaction. As you are on your own, there are no-one else's rules to follow, so you can eat however you like. You can follow your very own, wired-in conative need for eating in this personal eating scenario.

Your Chunks and Bits Processor is at its peak, weighing up whether to make one of those smoothies or just to cut off a sizeable chunk of freshly-made, apple cream sponge cake that's stored very conveniently in the refrigerator ... or even whether to tough it out until the next meal.

"Chunks and Bits" deduces that a smoothie is what's needed because healthy living is high on your values list. However, there is a proviso. Some cake will be okay later ... one medium sized piece when your friend comes over for dinner in the evening will be fine.

With that, the signal to proceed is given by your I-Will processor and the following sequence ensues:

1. Get out your smoothie recipe book.

2. Work out which of the three new temptations you short-listed last time will work best for you this time.

3. Cross-reference recipe ingredients with what's in the pantry and refrigerator.

4. Check that the smoothie maker is clean and operational.

5. Retrieve your special smoothie glass from the glass cabinet.

6. Gather all necessary ingredients.

7. Have your favourite long-handled spoon ready to scoop out the frothy bits sticking to the empty glass at the end.

8. Make the smoothie.

9. Sit on your cool front step with a satisfied gaze out at the great Aussie bush, sipping impeccable sips of the most exquisite, healthy, energy-boosting sensation of a smoothie you have ever tasted ... so sensational, you decide it will definitely be on top of the list for the next workout. "Maybe," you think, "It would even be a very good <u>habit</u> to get into."

There is however, one other scenario worth considering, and it's not a jogging one. Does this sound at all familiar?

"Feeling hungry!

Go to refrigerator

Get some cake

Mmmm!

And some of that unfinished chocolate

Mmmmm!

Oh yes, and some of that nice dark, "morish" fizzy drink.

Mmmmmmmmm!

Then go to lounge and eat ... facing big new plasma screen.

Then go back to the refrigerator for more cake and choc and fizz.

And maybe then go back and get even more cake and choc and fizz, and eat."

No thinking required - all fully automated "getting" and "eating."

Those were just two of the likely possibilities.

The different scenarios we could have chosen number as many as there are people on this planet, plus more. Every one of us is unique with different emotional sets, different IQ's, different physical capabilities, different conative needs and different states of spiritual reality.

What's great about these two scenarios is that they, together, make a point. They contrast two very different modes of human behaviour ... two different states of mental activity and two different sets of implications for our next set of actions, and the next and the next for the rest of our lives. In fact, these two examples could show us how we have chosen to live our lives from right back at its very beginning.

"How so?" you ask.

"How can we be so different as to engage in a healthy fruit smoothie on one hand and go for the slick sweetness of sponge cake and TV on the other?"

"As human beings, are we locked into this dilemma of choices forever or are there some parts inside of us, within the bio-mental energy cloud of our Critical Space that only <u>appear </u>fixed which are however, really quite changeable?"

The answers to these questions, we will discover, lie in a deeper inspection of these two seemingly ordinary, everyday examples.

What these two examples show us is a very clear and practical difference between a <u>conscious response</u> and an <u>unconscious habit.</u>

Let's dig into unconscious habits first.

They are the most common and easy to recognize of all human behaviours. We execute them. We harbour them. We nurture them. We love them. We fall for their seduction all the time. Is it any surprise that they are also very likely the most primitive and they have been studied scientifically or received formal comment across cultures and centuries, from Aristotle to Locke and Descartes to Patanjali?

Unconscious habits are with us all the time. Without them we could not live.

In more recent times, habits have come under the general discipline of Stimulus/Response Psychology and Behaviourism.

Simple habits like blinking when that bee did a crazy fly-by up close and personal in your face, like your stinging, toddler hand flying away from the hot BBQ that somehow escaped your vigilance or like the spasms of uncontrollable shivering as you stood waiting numbly on a windy, -2°C bus stop at 11pm, are all stimulus/response situations. In terms of the E.C.R.O.M. idea, they are events and reactions in rapid sequence, engineered inside of your very own Critical Space.

There are other unconscious habits that are even more basic than these. They are still stimulus/response scenarios and we have encountered them briefly in the previous chapter where our Physical Energy processor was introduced i.e. our regular heartbeat and working of other vital organs, for example, lungs, brain, liver, bladder and kidneys, all of which work and work to keep us alive and doing what we do. Every one of these organs, and many others, harness this exact simple and repetitive neuro-chemical pattern. In science it's called a reflex arc. Our cells are stimulated by some threatening change in their environment and send out signals to our central nervous system (brain and spinal cord). Our central nervous system, as a result and <u>without</u> engaging any other mental processors, immediately sends out similar impulses to the organs to maintain control and restore our overall stability. The heart muscles are signalled to relax or contract, the liver to adjust the release of stored energy food into our blood stream, our chest and back muscles (for shivering) to get fired up very smartly and stay fired up to help keep our body temperature in the safe range.

Reflex arcs form a truly awesome and vital control system happening inside each one of us every moment of our waking and sleeping lives.

Can life-sustaining, neuro-chemical habits like these be changed? Do we have any control over them at all?

"Yes" and "Yes," though it's sometimes not easy and often a challenge.

Just as the chemistry and electricity of our inner physiology allows this internal micro-communication to happen, so too is it electrochemistry that can intervene, thanks to the cleverness, precision-technology and power of modern medical science.

Our central nervous system has the brief of delivering a stable inner environment free of major upsets, the brief of maintaining in balance, a set of the most intricate, miraculous, life-sustaining variables imaginable ... and it follows this job description impeccably.

For reasons that continue to keep our researchers hard at work though, our central nervous system sometimes gets out of sync with the organs it works so closely with. In these instances, drugs and electro-chemical procedures are administered to help out ... for most people that is. For insulin-dependent diabetics, for example, chemical intervention is a fact of life and it is just "par for their daily course." It is woven inextricably into their lifestyles.

Very, very many casualties of cardio-vascular disease and other traumatic accidents have dodged the "death bullet" and been given a second chance by the timely deployment of a handy defibrillator, a portable electric device for restoring normal heart rhythm.

Chemical inhalants continue to soothe and restore normal breathing for thousands of asthmatics on this planet daily. The list of intervening chemicals and procedures goes on and on ... more than enough to fill all the pages in this book.

On a more non-electrochemical note, there are credible accounts from antiquity, and in more recent times, observed and documented accounts of solitary individuals who have defied the odds. With raw discipline and unflinching dedication to mastery over their physical bodies, they have been able at will, to speed up, slow down or even stop their heart beat.

They have likewise been able to suspend operation of all of their other life-sustaining systems and shift themselves into a state of controlled suspended animation. These individuals are the avatars, the shamans, the yogis and yoginis, the saints and the healers of legend and literature. They are the short-list of exceptional beings among the billions that have walked this earth since we first started asking ourselves about ourselves. They have led us and taught us, healed us and inspired us, silently challenging us at every turn: "If I can learn and do this, then you could learn and do some of it too. It will make your world and the world of others a better place."

Gandhi said of Christ, "In the lesson of His own life, Jesus gave humanity the magnificent purpose and the single objective towards which we all aught to aspire." (Paramahansa Yogananda *"The Autobiography of a Yogi"* 2007 p. 378)

Shri Nisargartta Maharaj, a twentieth century yogi of a distinguished lineage delivers a similar message even more succinctly, "Know yourself correctly. There is no substitute for self-knowledge."

Let's now turn our attention a little closer to our habits.

The fridge-cake-TV scenario represents a habit because it has two simple qualities:

1. The action is automatic or partly automatic ... not much thinking or pondering happens, if any happens at all.

2. The sequence of actions has happened before, more than once, i.e. it is repeated behaviour.

Let's say for convenience, that the fridge-cake-TV sequence has been repeated many times. It is a habit. The type of cake and what's on TV may have been different, that's all.

Can we change this kind of habit?

"Yes, absolutely." And some serious pointers on how we can do that, you will find later in this work in Part Two. For now though, it's enough to know that on the very first round of fridge-cake-TV eating, your hunger was satisfied in the most pleasant of ways for you ... your "sweet tooth" was satisfied. Your Feelings processor grabbed that terrifically satisfying feeling when you finished the first wedge of cake and stored it in your subconscious memory banks. It was a winner! On top of that came the pleasant and timely reinforcement of the television. All you had to do was press a button on the remote to get the channel that made you feel even more comfy and then sit back with your sweet, pleasure-hit and enjoy. You instantly became part of the action ... next to no effort required. Again, this bonus serving of fortified TV pleasure was scooped up and recorded in your subconscious along with the cake memory. What then, made this all happen again so effortlessly? There is a connector ... a trigger to make it happen over and over and over again. In this case, it is simply feeling hungry <u>and</u> being close to that wonderfully reliable source of gastronomical satisfaction, the refrigerator. The image and feeling of the refrigerator, by the way, also gets wrapped for storage with the cake and the TV tucked away, out of mind until next time, when another hunger event gets registered and the cycle begins again.

Though it will come out in more detail in Part Two of this book, it's worth knowing at this point that to change this kind of habit requires only one thing. It requires a reason to change for without a reason, why would you go to some other inconvenient place for a great taste and why would you bother finding some other inconvenient place to sit that mightn't be anywhere near as comfortable and entertaining? The habit will only change when either the pleasure dries up and you get bored or you spot an even easier way to get the pleasure happening, one that's even more comfortable and entertaining (or both). Habits like these, where our comfort is at stake, can either takes us down the disease track or they can work for us and serve us if we let them. As we shall see in Part Two, we can become construction and reconstruction engineers of our own habits, especially the "fridge-cake-TV" ones.

Well engineered, well maintained and well-groomed habits are some of our most powerful allies.

It's time now to revisit the smoothie.

Relaxing into the sensation of good living, satisfaction, health and vitality after the workout is not an automatic reaction. It is not a habit yet!

So, how is the "smoothie" response different from the "fridge-TV" reaction?

It is different in one important way. Arrival on your favourite front step with the "health-kick" of a drink involved a lot of conscious mind-space, remembering, weighing up your want against your need, considering the background of your values, what you believe and the rules and standards to which you yourself have committed. These too, like the mental tools and processors that hold and sustain them, are inside of you, in your mind, and they occupy an apparently huge portion of your Critical Space.

These values and beliefs and rules for doing what you do, have been set up over your lifetime ... since the instant you drew your first breath and, if they include a belief in the esoteric and in reincarnation, then even before that ... in your mother's womb and further back in previous lifetimes.

Some time in your life (or pre-life), through a deliberate or inadvertent set of circumstances, you acquired a value concerning good health, vitality and fitness and now you believe, without question, that it's a good thing to value. You have also developed some aides, either deliberately or accidentally, so that this admirable belief can be sustained on a daily basis. You have made up a set of standards about eating and references and rules to help you stay on your healthy eating track. These values and beliefs and standards are the stuff of your Critical Space ... of everyone's Critical Space. It is where your mental processors infuse them into your every action, your every thought and your every feeling.

Taking a more close-up look at the "smoothie" response, remember that your Chunks and Bits processor doesn't work too well with raw emotion. It needs the certainty of facts and figures. A crystal-clear definition with no grey areas is good. The standards and personal benchmarks you created to support those values and beliefs add an even more agreeable dimension to the Chunks and Bits workspace.

Values, beliefs and standards represent a level of certainty for Chunks and Bits to deal with the ups and downs of life.

Valuing great health and believing whole fresh food is good for you is what we're talking about here.

Within your Critical Space also, is a very powerful and influential "gut feeling." It is a deep, instinctive, intuitive knowing of what's best for you and which is the true essence of your I-Will processor. Your Chunks and Bits processor includes this in its weigh-up too.

It is the same for where you chose to eat ... a front step with a nature view ... a place that reflects other values and beliefs of yours to do with nature and spiritual communion with it.

To settle on the smoothie rather than the chocolate cake required some serious engagement of your great Mental Energy processors. "Fridge-TV" won the day as a <u>reaction</u> and habit in the previous example because most of the action was taken over by "thought-less" emotion. "Hungry" equals "eat with maximum satisfaction."

"Smoothie" wins the <u>response</u> game, mostly as a result of collaboration between your Chunks and Bits processor (Cognitive) and your I-Will processor (Conative). They don't exactly gang up on your Feelings processor (Affective), they just provide an energy off-set, a counterbalance or a brake, an equalizer to keep you going where you need to go.

Having said that, your Feelings processor does have an important and integral role to play. After all, feeling is about gratification of your desires. It's about staying alive, not being eaten by sharks. In this case, it's gratification with a twist, gratification that's been tamed and brought to heel through a conscious and engineered deployment of your mental and physical energies. It is delayed. You postponed your eating satisfaction by putting in time and conscious effort to make the smoothie.

In arriving at the front step, gazing out at the great Aussie bush and downing an exquisitely healthy smoothie, you have engaged all of your processors in a more even distribution of your total mental energy. The fridge-TV scenario pretty well gave it all up to your Feeling processor.

So how, you may well ask, does this one-off <u>response</u> get turned into a habit?

Just as it takes a reason to break the sub-conscious fridge-TV habit, so too does a conscious habit need the power and the motivation of a great reason for its creation. You might think this, "I will do this after my workouts every time, from now on. That feeling as I cross the finish line of the 10k fun run I pulled out of last year (because I was over-weight) will be so sweetly satisfying!"

You will notice that "feeling" is right in there with "motivation" and "power" to do or change something. Remember that feelings (emotions) are the fuel for doing what you do.

Big reason + heaps of emotional fuel in your Critical Space = You move mountains = You make and break habits. This example is for a simple eating habit. The formula however, is the same for more sophisticated habits like reading and adding, multiplying and dividing, writing and competitive high jumping.

Only two ingredients remain in order to transform this singular, one-off, impeccable, smoothie-sipping into a fully-fledged and useful habit.

Repetition and reinforcement must happen. The more repetition and the more intense the positive "feelings" reinforcement is, the more ingrained and powerful the habit.

To round off this chapter on reacting or responding in *"Decisions, Decisions!"* let's take a third and final scenario. It's a common one with which you will no doubt be familiar.

Let's say it's 6:30am, your alarm has just gone off and you are mostly conscious and enjoying an agreeable "lie-in."

It's nice in there ... just the right temperature ... not too much light and it's soothingly quiet.

Ahead of you is a full day with some easy "stuff" up first and maybe a stretch of "hard yards" later on, depending on how you "shaped up" in the morning.

Now you would just love to max out on the comfort and squeeze in a few more minutes of this soft and seductive space of sleepy reverie. Staying too long, you know, will definitely squash the day into an uncomfortable, devastating rush ... not the best for appearances and certainly not good for your trademark efficiency, yet getting out of bed right now would rob you of some very precious "me" time. After all, you do your share of voluntary, unpaid overtime in that establishment as a loyal company supporter. You deserve a little longer.

Then suddenly, without thinking, you find yourself on your feet, pulling the bed clothes to order and neatness and getting yourself groomed and set up for the day. A moment before, you were horizontal and comfortable under the linen and now you are in full action mode ... from soft comfy bed to shiny angular mirrors and tiles in the bathroom. It's all good though. You cruise through your grooming and pre-departure routine, arrive at work on time, "eat up" the easy morning session and shape up admirably for the tricky bit in the afternoon. It has been a great day for you.

There is a piece in this seemingly ordinary everyday episode worth elaborating on and it's a piece of "neuro-machinery" in your mental workshop. It is the trigger that got you out of bed and sent you forth with such dedicated intent ... the switch that turned your motor on and thrust you into the new day. It is the same switch that is flicked every single time you step across that imaginary line between mental and physical action ... between your intention to do and action (or inaction) that follows. It is where the dynamic pulse of deciding moves from your Critical Space to one of reaction or response ... where your I-Will processor discharges the starter's gun and you begin your race.

How does "it" know when to pull the trigger?

The signal to do is given when your personal threshold of pain or intolerance is reached ... when you cannot bear, for one second or one split second longer, the pain or discomfort you feel inside.

Do other processors have a hand in all of this?

Yes, they most certainly do.

We can safely say your Chunks and Bits system did the debating bit, all the rapid-fire to-ing and fro-ing and all the weighing up of the pros and cons of sneaking some extra moments in bed and why you should stay there and why you shouldn't.

Also, locked away in your unconscious memory register of significant moments, was one small interlude of pain and disappointment you had completely forgotten about, until now that is, because it was particularly embarrassing and undermining of your fragile self-esteem at the time. It might also have something to do with the fact that it was mostly your own doing.

When you were fourteen years old, you missed your big chance to go and see live, your number one, no-one-is-better-than-this group of rock stars ... your global gurus of rock, doing their magic the way you love it, with your best friends.

You missed that show!

How could you have done such a thing?!!!

Simple, you slept in and missed the train ... no more to be said. No need to rub more salt into that still gaping wound however, that memory did some fine work for you today. It gave you a breeze of a day ... a day that could have easily gone the other way had your Feelings processor not loaded up your internal emotional combustion chamber to ignition point.

Pain, disappointment, embarrassment and many, many other emotional "fuels" do that. They work for us in order to avoid more pain next time. It's the way we're built.

The energy inflow from the painful memory of that soul-destroying rock event was enough to trip the switch in your I-Will processor and launch you into the safe haven of being in control and enjoying a great day.

As well as tipping you over the edge, out of a state of passive indulgence, I-Will laid out most of what came next, the bed clothes, neatness and order, the grooming and after that, all the times in your day where you happily made progress because you were able to work in the "stress-less" way you needed to.

Of course, it works the other way too, with positive emotion, the promise and lure of a great party on the weekend or being in the first five over the line in the 150k bike ride or the A+ for your final assignment. These powerful positives pull us forwards from the front. They draw us onwards as if we are being pulled along on a giant bungee cord.

So with pain prodding from behind and pleasure of amazingly numerous varieties pulling and beckoning and coaxing from the front, and with a mental I-Will trigger poised in between, we are moved to do ... to unconsciously react or to consciously respond in every decision we make.

How a little conscious engineering can help make those decisions the right ones, we shall discover in Part Two.

Check out these dot point nuggets. They really are the nitty-gritty of how we behave.

CH 3 FOR THE DOT POINTERS

Reaction or Response

- **Taking action or not taking action is either an unconscious reaction or a conscious response.**

- **Your reactions and your responses happen according to how your mental processors set them up.**

- Your five mental energy processors collaborate to determine the nature of every one of your reactions and every one of your responses.

- Repetitive patterns of reacting are called habits.

- Reflex arcs are basic stimulus-response habits. They never involve conscious processing.

- Reflex-arc energy keeps our physical systems operating and maintained at safe levels.

- Normally we have very limited natural control over our reflex arcs.

- Some drugs and medications modify reflex arc activity to medical advantage. It may not always work one hundred percent.

- Saints, yogis and gifted healers seem to be able to control their physical systems through rigorous, prolonged, mental and physical practices.

- To change a habit only requires a big enough <u>reason</u> to do so, some <u>application</u> and <u>practice</u>.

- A conscious response happens when the five mental processors in your Critical Space collaborate to set you up for conscious action or conscious in-action.

- Your values, beliefs and standards are integral to this mental collaboration.

- A one-off conscious response can become a habit by repeating it with emotional reinforcement and practice.

- Your Critical Space harbours a tipping point for emotional energy where a mental trigger sparks an unconscious reaction or a conscious response.

- This mental trigger is part of your I-Will (Conative) processor.

- Emotional energy that reaches your emotional threshold and activates the mental trigger can build up either through painful acts or memories or through anticipated pleasurable events or both.

- Painful, conscious or unconscious memories drive your reactions and responses from behind. Anticipation of pleasurable events pulls you along from the front.

O

CHAPTER 4

O - OUTCOME

CHAPTER 4

O - YOUR OUTCOME IS YOUR DESTINATION. IT IS WHERE YOU'RE HEADED.

Make sure it's exactly where you want to go.

As the headline of this chapter says, the outcome of a decision you make is where you are headed when you first commit to taking action from that point of commitment to <u>do</u> (something).

At that point your I-Will starter gun went off and you were immediately headed for an outcome. Whether or not you got there and <u>how</u> you did or didn't get there, depends on whatever happened in your Critical Space before the gun went off.

If you knew from the outset precisely what you wanted to achieve or exactly where you wanted to go, then chances are you have arrived right there, conclusively on target and with a feeling of satisfaction that you will have claimed another certainty in your life's journey ... a great result!

Let's take a look at a simple example of an outcome for ease of understanding. You have been feeling "down in the dumps" for a few days. Your friends have noticed and have been kind and tolerant however, you've overheard the odd comment to the effect you are below par and should be approached with sensitivity and a little caution.

You know things aren't right and you also know the reason. It's because you've got a mega tax bill this financial year and the return has to be done by the end of the month. This year you've been a bit behind with the paperwork and have procrastinated, leaving only two weeks to the deadline. It all gets too much to bear. That emotional threshold is reached and you make a commendable admission, you admit to yourself that maybe you were a just bit slack and you commit to removing the pain. You will tackle your paperwork blues head on, deciding not to make it all disappear temporarily with a session of intoxication at the local (pub). Instead, you take a few quiet and uninterrupted moments to collect your thoughts and commit, on paper, to some serious action.

By Friday of the first week remaining, you will have all relevant bank statements assembled and organised, you will have determined private use of the business vehicle, you will have worked out the phone and internet costs you missed recording for the two months you were overseas and you will have accounted for income and expenditure that doesn't attract goods and services tax.

In the second week you will have extracted and collated all relevant figures from the above and other documents under the headings your accountant requested for his part in the operation: Sales, Other Income, Bank Interest, Loan Repayments, Expenses, Value of Stock, Bad Debts, etc. You will deliver the same to him by 3:00pm on the Thursday of that second week. This is one day before time because you've been caught before and now know how valuable simple contingency planning can be. Just to be thorough, you will also call your bookkeeping friend who owes you a favour to double-check you haven't missed anything important.

Did you make it?

Yes you did. It turned out to be a little irksome at times retrieving misplaced data, with some anxious moments and uncomfortable, late night stretches. The delivery to your accountant happened on the Friday. You did need that extra day.

Great contingency planning!

Well done you!

And as for the mega tax bill ... you decided to just take that one "on the chin," pay it when it turns up and get on with your life.

You most certainly did make it all happen and you felt all the emotions of satisfaction a completed tax return can deliver to someone so careful, diligent and as hard working as yourself.

Let's imagine for a moment now, that it wasn't you "down in the dumps."

Let's say it was someone you know and who believes the whole tax system is a rort and a conspiracy. "It's run by a "mob" whose right hand doesn't know what its left is doing and it exists only to "hammer" the everyday worker and business owner into the ground." This un-named, reluctant, "tax-oppressed" citizen has the same two weeks left to get his tax act sorted as you did.

How did he fare?

The job is still not done. The overdue notice from the tax office is on its way.

After a fortnight of directionless ranting and wallowing, this acquaintance of yours is even more unattractive to hang out with than before.

You don't see him much these days.

Same job ... same deadline two ... completely different outcomes.

What makes these outcomes so different are the tools, the materials and the procedures at work in yours and "that other guy's" mental space.

Your mental workshop was set up for your accountant to have that information on his desk on time, at three o'clock on Friday afternoon. Your mental energy was well-deployed by your "team" of well-coordinated, Critical Space, energy processors. You were headed in the right direction from the moment you made the first move to get the job done i.e. from those few moments of uninterrupted time-out before putting your plan into action. Sure, you lost a day. You "sensed" from the outset that something might get in the way and you covered that base well. Had you focused on that "something" from the start, then maybe the two-hour dental appointment you didn't write in your diary and completely forgot about would have surfaced from your subconscious in time and allowed you to correct your schedule and meet your preferred Thursday deadline.

In the second case, the acquaintance that's not you, the one you don't see much of these days, was being groomed by his Critical Space in the same way, yet for a quite different road. His mental workshop set him up on a different course. Instead of a timely submission of tax information to his accountant, he focused on beating the system.

From the outset, his course was one of emotional attack on an "unjust system." He set out facing in a totally different direction from you, a direction determined by a set of beliefs about taxation, rules about who's responsible for what and very likely some beliefs about his relationships with all other "not-Tax-Office" people, including his partner and close family.

In both scenarios, between the starter's gun sounding in the Critical Space to take action and the tax information arriving (or not arriving) on the accountant's desk, there was a string of decisions made (or not made) to keep the whole operation happening, an uncountable number in fact, of mini decisions, every one with an inbuilt potential to derail, sabotage, undermine or side-track if some conscious monitoring and constructive, subconscious conditioning wasn't practised. What matters is how much self-correction happens in this space of execution and how much time and mental and physical energy is put into asking the questions:

"How am I going?"

"Do I need to change anything to reach my objective?"

"Am I running away from any of the hard bits?"

So far we've seen what an outcome looks like in the flesh i.e. the actual manifestation of what your Critical Space creates ... the tax figures delivered to the accountant's desk or opening the "overdue" tax office notice.

Now there is a bit more to these hypotheticals and it applies not just to hypotheticals: It applies to every decision that's ever been made by every person throughout all of history and into the future as well ... for as long as we keep choosing and deciding. That's probably a very long time. The "more" bit refers to what goes on in your Critical Space the moment you reach your objective (or don't reach it). After all, your Critical Space is still there in its ever-present, invisible glory, taking in events, filtering events, registering events and storing them as memories in your conscious and subconscious memory banks. It continues to be the mental workshop or the dressing room, wielding the power of co-ordination and distribution of precious mental energy amongst your five great processors: Chunks and Bits (Cognitive), Feelings (Affective), I-Will (Conative), Physical (Psychomotor) and Me (Spiritual).

Your Critical Space does this constantly.

At the moment you experience your very own pre-determined outcome, your Chunks and Bits processor has retrieved and posted in your mental workshop or dressing room, a virtual frieze or time-line of facts and figures, chunks and bits of identifiable information, packages of certainty. This mental collage is a totally brand new mental arrangement. Sometimes it may be as small and as insignificant as selecting chop sticks instead of a fork with which to eat your stir fry or the myriad of unconscious, rapid-fire and fleeting calculations where you chose to flick an ant from your sleeve instead of swatting it with your folded newspaper. This outcome, this finished mental picture you now have in your memory banks, is new and it is unique. It means your cognitive "you" has changed forever. In your memory banks now is one more spanking new package of cognitive, mental energy, at the ready for deployment should it be needed for any future decisions.

With change of any kind comes a new energy state, however small or exhilaratingly enormous. The cognitive "you" at the outcome end of a decision is not the same cognitive "you" as at the start. The same applies for your other processors which have also loyally processed their way through their own respective changes, changes that have blended with Chunks and Bits to collaboratively produce a total new, big-picture energy state ... a totally new "you" state.

Your Feelings processor will have bathed you in a state of satisfaction of a job well done, a happy accountant, a decision well made or, for that 'other chap,' a bath of ranting anger wrapped in blame and venom against an outside, unfeeling, ruthless, oppressive taxation entity.

The satisfaction you feel at the goal posts will be a new kind of satisfaction, one with the frills and trappings of the unique event that started it all in the first place, all inside your Critical Space. The satisfaction of triumphantly overcoming the mental pain and the anxiety and frustration of getting that daunting tax return delivered is now wrapped around a memory reference-point, coloured with emotional energy and powerfully anchoring it as a reminder of what you, as a great operator, can do. Such are the strange and diverse wrappings of pain!

Now, at the end of the two "tax" weeks, your physical energy may well match the elation you feel and you are ready to take on, let's say, a half-marathon or it could be much depleted because you got stressed-out reformatting your records the way your accountant wanted them i.e. you had to work against your I-Will (conative) grain. You couldn't do the job quite in the way you really needed to in the time you gave yourself. Either way, a complete record has been dutifully kept in your memory banks of all the conative activity that pushed you through to get the numbers done on time.

In your determination to stay true to your commitment, you also sacrificed fitness for time at the keyboard, entering data and checking the numbers.

Two routine physical weekly workouts did not happen. You skipped them in order to do the paperwork. In fact, you pushed yourself a little too far, compromised your immune system and ended the operation with a head cold. All this is stored away too, as memory for future reference. More references, more wrapping, more stored information.

On a spiritual note, you found yourself pondering over why you do this tax "stuff" at all?

"Why does anyone do it?"

You even thought, "Why do I do anything at all?"

"Maybe I could explore this question in depth, maybe read some books about the meaning of life and me and the universe and everything."

You even considered the notion that every moment of your life is an outcome of some decision you've made some time in the past; a second or two ago or maybe twenty years ago.

"Could it be," you pondered, "that's what living in the now is all about?"

Now, just in case you're asking, "Well, that's all very well and makes perfect sense. What about when the outcome isn't the one I had in mind ... like the other day, after I came in late to a meeting.

I realized I'd got my times mixed up, confessed to having made a mistake and was promptly reprimanded by my boss in front of the whole team for being unprofessional, disorganized, careless and irresponsible, and not what one would expect in a professionally run establishment. Or did he just get out of bed the wrong side that day?"

To find out, check through the dot points below and then read more about this hypothetical life you seem to have become party to in the next chapter of this book.

Now hook your bungee cord into these (pleasure-packed) dot points.

CH 4 FOR THE DOT POINTERS

Your Outcome is Your Destination - it's Where You're Headed

- **The outcome of a decision is determined by conscious and unconscious activity in your Critical Space.**

- **The instant action on a decision is taken, you are headed for a particular, predetermined outcome.**

- **Even without conscious monitoring and self-correction of the action taken, the outcome set up in your Critical Space will happen.**

- **The action taken on a decision is driven by the combined activity of your five mental energy processors. The mental energy processors draw on your conscious and sub-conscious memory banks to formulate the action plan.**

- The outcome you want, or prefer or hope for, is not always the outcome you get.

- The action plan set up in your Critical Space has a conscious and subconscious component. The unconscious component is hidden from your awareness and can steer the action away from the outcome you want or towards it without your being aware of it.

- The action phase of a decision you make is what some professionals would call the <u>execution</u> phase of the decision.

- Why the outcome you want and the outcome you get are sometimes different is answered in the next chapter.

M

CHAPTER 5

M - MEASURING THE OUTCOME

CHAPTER 5

M - ALWAYS MEASURE HOW CLOSE YOU GET TO YOUR INTENDED OUTCOME. IT'S YOUR RESULT AND RESULTS MATTER

So what's measurement got to do with making a decision ... with choosing this or that or that?

Measuring is crucial!

Without measurement, a decision can be worthless. In fact, it's hardly a decision at all without some degree of comparing what you had in mind with what actually happened.

When an event is registered in your Critical Space, a raw stimulus is allocated a meaning or an "unknown" is labelled "unfamiliar" or "uncertain." Your Critical Space powers on with or without the facts. It engages more stored mental energy and eventually comes up with a "story" for that event ... a collection of meanings and labels that make best sense of what you've experienced. Just how clear and bright that mental composition is, comes down to the tools and materials, the ingrained procedures and protocols already set up in your mental workshop or dressing room i.e. in your Critical Space. However this assemblage of meanings appears, it will be an impression or sensation or vision of what your life could be like at some time in the future, in five seconds, five days, five years or fifty. Your Critical Space has an amazing capacity to play its compositions forwards. When that time in the future arrives, is when measurement needs to happen and it is you and only you who does the measuring, either consciously or unconsciously.

If your mental workshop or dressing room has been kept spic and span, clear of off-cuts and clutter, swept clean of junk and your mental energy processors are in sync and harmony, then all's well.

"YAY!

I made it.

I'm here on time in the box seat, ready for my stars to come on stage, and it feels exactly right.

Great job!

Excellent planning!

Great execution!

I deserve this.

Thank you Universe."

Or is it like this,

"*#0'!!?*#^! This isn't how it's supposed to be.

What the *#0'!!?*#^! happened?"

Or maybe this:

"Well, we took a bit of a roundabout way ... a bit messy you might say however, we made it in the end. We could have gone left instead of straight ahead and saved a lot of time and energy ... too bad. We're here now ... let's get on with the job."

In every case, there was an outcome and in every case there was a result.

Terrific result: Your dream of seeing your rock "gurus" live, on stage, in style and at your favourite international destination came magnificently to fruition. You are a very, very, happy, satisfied camper. What you got equalled what you wanted, equals great result.

Not-so-terrific result: There are some serious "bugs and viruses" active in your mental workshop ... maybe some mental sawdust clogging the mental waste disposal ducts or some loose tools from the last job not put away and scattered around getting in the way or maybe some "theatre imps" in your mental dressing room or some sneaky mental "flies" in your mental "facial ointment" that you allowed in somewhere along the way without knowing.

What happened does not equal what you wanted, equals a not-so-terrific result.

Okay result: Not quite on target. We could have done better. No harm done though ... just a little behind schedule.

What happened approximately equalled what you wanted, equals "okay" result.

Now there is another scenario.

If, after the live show, you were invited back-stage to meet your rock "gurus'" lead performer, then your result is screaming off the score board in the positive. You achieved way beyond expectations. That was surely an extra bonus ... a magic moment. Some other factor, somewhere, was working for you ... an outstanding result!

So ... **knowing** that you've actually arrived at your outcome (or not arrived) is the first part of measuring.

The second part is comparing what actually happened with what you wanted or expected or believed you planned for (and remember, measurement counts because results count).

How close you got to what you wanted is your result.

An investment of dollars is usually meant to get a result, a positive one, an account "in the black," more money in the bank.

Dropping your line on this side of the boat and not the other for a catch is a decision that has a built-in expectation of an outcome, a legally sized fish you can put into your "bag." Anything less is an unsatisfactory result, especially if your livelihood depends on catching legally sized fish.

Measurement applies to the big decisions as well as the small ones.

Deciding to quit your job, to boil an egg for breakfast, to "shoo" a fly from your nose, will each grace you with an outcome and corresponding result should you choose to do some essential comparing.

What makes results count so much and what makes them so important, you will find in the pages of Part Two of this book. You will discover, for example, that it's about <u>what</u> you do with your result and exactly <u>how</u> you measured the difference between what happened and what you wanted, that determines the quality of your decision.

Now there is some important "nitty-gritty" of measurement that we must look at in the decision-making world. For example, what do you have to do to compare what you got with what you wanted?

And what do you actually use to do the measuring?

After all, when you measure up a sheet of ply or a length of hardwood in a carpenter's workshop, you use a ruler or a tape measure. To measure the time you need to get "made up" for your appearance in the second act of your performance, you would use your watch or a timer, mobile phone or the wall clock in the dressing room.

So, a great question to ask would be, "In your mental workshop or dressing room, what's the ruler or tape measure or clock or mobile phone for the measurement you make?"

And where exactly does this interesting device come from? Where is the tool rack or make-up drawer or mental vanity unit where it is kept?

This small punch-packing, mental, measuring device, this indispensable mental tool that can measure with exquisite engineering precision, has the simplicity of a short question. In fact it is a question.

The question is, "Is this what I wanted?"

"Is this what I planned?"

"Is this what I dreamed of?"

Take your pick. Only one is needed.

And then just to be thorough, ask another equally short and critical question, "If it isn't what I wanted, how far off the mark am I?"

Mental measuring is simply asking these two short questions.

And where, you ask, do these two harmless looking movers and shakers come from? Where, in your mental workshop or dressing room, are they kept for such easy retrieval?

Answer: In the refined, masterful, well-groomed and organized mental energy mesh of your Chunks and Bits processor. That's where!

Asking questions is what your Chunks and Bits processor does, all the time. It's what it was designed for. It is the arch-questioner of all time, the mental guru in your Critical Space that has moved the human race since it appeared on planet earth, from the Neolithic nomads to New Age nerds, from cavemen to connoisseurs. Your Chunks and Bits processor never stops asking questions and should you choose to allow it, it will even subdivide its questions into infinitesimally small, dendritic, mini-questions that allow you to measure your success even more precisely.

Is your Chunks and Bits processor the only source of measurement?

Is there somewhere else where mental rulers and timers and speedos and bathroom scales are stored?

Yes indeed.

Not only are they stored, they're in operation constantly, automatically and unconsciously.

Yes, parts of you are being measured all the time and you aren't even aware of it.

In Chapter Two about your Critical Space and Physical Energy processor, we were introduced to your autonomic nervous system, that neuro-system of every human being that fires continually, often in dashes at near-lightning speed that keeps you alive.

To bring your temperature down after a gruelling workout or slow your heart rate after a scare on the highway, engages a whole 'basketful' of your automatic, unconscious measurers.

And the measurer itself?

The measurer is a point of sharp, highly evolved intelligence that we each have. At near lightning speed it reads the continuous, incoming flood of neuro-signals from every cell in your body, compares each one of them to a built-in reference point and then deploys instructions to correct and adjust. Your temperature comes down because your skin has been instructed to let out more water for cooling evaporation, your heartbeat drops very soon after the signal to cut adrenalin supply reaches your adrenal glands, all silently accomplished, automatically and masterfully done.

And what, you may rightfully ask, is this highly-evolved point of intelligence?

What is this reference point of invisible intelligence and where is it located?

This reference point is the point of singular intelligence in each of us called life or life-force and it exists physically in our brain. So far, all clues and research evidence points to a small area deep within our brain called the <u>hypothalamus</u>. The hypothalamus constantly monitors our life-support system. Life only happens when conditions are just right. Anything that's outside the "life zone" is immediately picked up by our hypothalamus with speed, efficiency and precision. It then instantly corrects and puts us back on the life track and in the "safe" zone. If the correction isn't made for whatever reason, then life (ours) is threatened i.e. we could die. The safe human operating temperature for example, is 37°C. Anything above or below that level flashes a red alert in the hypothalamus. A true measure of the difference is made and corrections carried out and they are kept in place until the threat is removed. How's that for measurement?

On a less microscopic scale, **measuring happens automatically in a big way when our "fight-or-flight" switch is turned on.** Remember the brown snake in chapter 2, when you were jogging along beside the river?

Snake! ... venom ... pain of death ... lots of fear ... bring on the adrenalin ... now!

Legs ... body ... move ... fast. Get out of here ... instantly, if not, sooner!

Your risk level went from "safe-jogging-with-iPod-connected-to-ear" to heart-thumping, high-risk, escape mode.

Thank you memory for storing away that little snippet ... "people can die of snake bite." That reminder was driven, with lasting impact into your subconscious by shear repetition as you were growing up, by your parents, teachers and other seniors who knew best and everything about the danger of snakes.

Your emotional transformation from "safe" to "serious risk," from "life-enhancement" to "life threat," from "reverie" to "high alert" in what seemed a split second, did not go unnoticed. The change was measured and addressed precisely by your shining inner star, neuro-intelligent singularity for life preservation, your hypothalamus.

So, mental mind-space measurement is with us all the time. It's been with us, and most other forms of animalia, since life began on the planet "xyz" million years ago.

If you are a physiologist or neuro-scientist or zoologist or biologist or any other "ologist" you would directly link this life balancing act to homeostasis. It is this life-balancing, neuro-chemical system that keeps us functioning, alive and healthy.

Just to recap for a moment: measurement of this kind must have a standard level or reference point, a benchmark to use as a comparison.

Now, believe it or not, every one of us has a whole room-full of these benchmarks and standards in our mental work space.

Again, they are mostly subconscious ones, maybe not buried as deep down as our neurological life-balance benchmarks of homeostasis, yet they are always at the ready for deployment to keep us on track and alive.

These are the big reference points of behaviour, our beliefs and our rules for doing what we do and thinking what we think.

Unlike the molecular, near-lightning-speed impulse networks of our autonomic nervous system, these are standards and benchmarks that we have learned or collected, sometimes unintentionally, from the moment of our first breath (or maybe even before that).

For example: "Snakes are dangerous." "The world hates me." "Nature is full of deadly creatures." "I never go into the garden at night unless I can see where I'm going." "Money doesn't grow on trees." "There is no God." "God loves me no matter what."

Just how these beliefs and in-grained stories of habit work with making decisions, we will explore soon in Part 2.

For now though, let's recap on this phenomenal capability of ours to measure what actually happens against what "should" have happened in this great decision-making playing field we call life ... check out the cartoon first though.

CH 5 FOR THE DOT POINTERS

Measurement

- **Without measurement, a decision can be worthless.**

- **Measurement compares what you got with what you wanted.**

- **The difference between what you got and what you wanted is your <u>result.</u>**

- **Conscious monitoring of the action you take and self-correction increases the chance of a great result.**

- No difference = Great result. Big difference = Not-great result.

- Results count and measurement counts because some decisions are life and death decisions.

- Some measurement happens unconsciously and is part of unconscious decision-making.

- Unconscious decisions and unconscious measurement happens via your automatic nervous system and via your ingrained habits of thought and action.

- Your automatic nervous system decides and measures to keep you in the safe life-zone.

- The safe life-zone is checked and maintained by your life-balance system or <u>homeostasis</u>.

- Your beliefs set your rules for your thinking and your actions.

- All measurement must have a measuring tool and a reference point against which to compare.

- Your mental measuring tool is your life-balance intelligence system.

- A part of your life-balance measurement happens deep within the brain, between the very top of your central spinal cord and the rest of your brain. It's called the <u>hypothalamus.</u>

- **Your measuring reference points are your unconscious life-balance standards, (like your core temperature of 37°C housed in your hypothalamus) and your unconscious habits of behaviour and thinking that you learn or accidentally acquire in the process of growing up.**

- **Your values, beliefs and rules are your measuring reference points for how you think and how you behave.**

PART II

THE PRACTICAL BIT

PART II

TRANSITION

Get ready now for a transition, a change where you must switch mental energy from soaking up new information, some of which you will have learned and already stored in your vast, internal memory banks. The next stage is about applying the E.C.R.O.M. idea to a whole lot of situations, most of which will be familiar because they happen to most of us all the time.

To switch mental gears and to be ready to soak up some useful application, please ask yourself these questions, "If I were to use the E.C.R.O.M. idea in my decision making from this point forwards, how would I use it? How could I use it to improve my business or home life?

How much better would relationships with family and colleagues be? How much better would my life be if I applied the E.C.R.O.M. idea to my decision making?"

Or an even simpler question, "How can the E.C.R.O.M. idea serve me in whatever I do?"

Time now to read on.

If you just want to sit on everything and "ruminate" for a while, to pause and think about what you've just taken on board and let the E.C.R.O.M. idea sink in, that's okay.

Part Two will be there, ready when you are.

WHAT'S IN PART TWO

Part One was about the parts and pieces that make up a decision, the E.C.R.O.M. idea, where **E** is a particular **Event**, **C** is your **Critical Space** or mental workshop or dressing room where mental processing happens, **R** is the **Reaction or Response** you make after the processing, **O** is the **Outcome** or what happens after you react or respond and **M** is the **Measurement** you apply to compare what you got in the end with what you wanted at the start. Your *result* is that comparison.

Part One is the <u>knowledge</u> section.

Part Two is the <u>practical application</u> and <u>trouble-shooting</u> section. It's about putting the E.C.R.O.M. idea to work, so that you can make better decisions and ultimately enjoy a more satisfying life. It's a run-through, if you like, of using the E.C.R.O.M. decision making blueprint to get something you want or need or dream of having or dream of being. It's the how-to-make-the-right-decision-every-time part, with some hot tips on getting started to make this new knowledge work for you. It's also the "What's-in-it-for-Me"(the reader) part.

So Part Two starts with the question, **"What makes a decision a right decision?"**

There's a **"Mess or Meaning?"** chapter that poses another very important question, **"Is what's not working for me really a mess and a failure or is it something else? Is it an opportunity to do something differently?"** Is it an opportunity to come up with some new meanings to old "stuff" that will serve me rather than be the roadblock it has been?

Next, there's a section that uses **the E.C.R.O.M. idea to "debug" and recondition your decision making machinery**. It's about working over your event identification and registration system and about reconditioning each of the mental workshops in your critical space (and this comes with an extra, <u>free</u>, bonus Critical Space companion e-book designed to supercharge your own reconditioning experience), then there's a chapter about quality control of your mental and physical reaction and response machinery and finally, some tips on honing your outcome-comparison skills so that you can more effectively measure for your result.

It's vital to get the E.C.R.O.M. solution working for you because not fixing what's broken down or out of sync, especially in your mind space, means eventually losing sight of that ultimate state you so keenly desire ... that dream ... your "bucket-list" objectives ... your life's mission. It would be like the engine of your motor vehicle running on contaminated fuel and ignoring the potential risk. Without pinpointing exactly what's not right for you, every decision you make will be tainted or contaminated in some way, from the automatic, unconscious, micro-chemical, homeostatic, adjustment decisions of your central nervous system, through to the ones which you've hopefully already made for this lifetime and which you won't have to endure again.

There's a neat section on using the E.C.R.O.M. Solution to consistently get where you really want to go or to get away from wherever you don't want to be.

To make any decision, you have to want something in the first place.

Being <u>proactive</u> and <u>focused</u> in deciding exactly what you're after is <u>the</u> most important part of getting it, all neatly summarised in the **Ten Rules for Making the Right Decision Every Time.**

Having "debugged" your mental workshops and dressing rooms and established clarity on what you want, you must keep the tidiness and clarity happening to make life even better than before the "clean-up." So there's a **"staying-on-track"** section.

Staying on track is really a fancy way of measuring "on the run," a way of keeping tabs on outcomes as they happen in order to make intelligent corrections along the way.

Finally, no book would be finished without a **concluding word**. There is a concluding word in this book and as the reader, you are part of it. In fact, you are the final word. You can go straight there if you can't wait or simply read on and take it as it comes.

Get set now for the nuts and bolts of Part Two.

FOR THE DOT POINTERS

What's in Part Two?

- **What makes a decision a right decision?**

- **"Debugging" and reconditioning your decision-making machinery, working on what needs working on, giving the old "mess" a new meaning, clearing out mental clutter and unhelpful habits and fixing what needs to be fixed so that you can confidently and efficiently move on in your life by asking the question, "Is this a mess or an opportunity for giving a new meaning to old stuff?" (Of course, this chapter comes with an accompanying _free_, downloadable, companion e-book at: _www.howtomaketherightdecisioneverytime.com_)**

- **The Ten Rules for Making the Right Decision Every Time: A summary of how to get an outstanding result every time.**

- **Staying on track with right measurement: What comes after the mental overhaul and being prepared for the unexpected.**

- **Concluding Word: Your Ultimate Decision (Check it out now in the last chapter if you like, or read on).**

CHAPTER 6

WHAT MAKES A DECISION A RIGHT DECISION?

CHAPTER 6

WHAT MAKES A DECISION A RIGHT DECISION?

(Am I Making Right Decisions?)

A right decision is a decision that you make and a decision that you own ... totally.

Owning a decision means taking responsibility for it in its entirety, no matter what.

That means claiming the outcome and the result as an extension of the driving force, conscious or unconscious, that created it ... your driving force, your conscious, your unconscious.

In a right decision, the driving force, the outcome and the measured result of the decision, are all part of you and of no other person or organization or universe.

On a lighter and more detailed note, there are an endless number of decisions that make up your world, some tiny and unconscious and others conscious and mountain-sized, with a vast range in between those two extremes. The personal "patch" you call your own world is the sum total of every decision you've ever made ... one after another, after another, after another. They are all linked in sequence, from the point of your first breath to right now. Some would even say before your first breath and others even way before that. We saw in Part One how your Critical Space was the mastermind for making your every decision ... conscious or unconscious, and we will revisit that bit a little later.

We have also seen, that for every decision, there is an invisible carrier or vehicle on which it rides. That vehicle is the drive or need to get something, to fly, like the attractive force of opposite magnetic poles, closer to something glorious or a desire to get away from something causing us grief, to flee with the repulsive intensity of like poles of the same two magnets, away from that which we do not want.

For example, let's say you decide to get out of your comfy bed to let the cat outside.

It's 2 am and it is cold. You don't even know there's ice on the steel fence railing in the front yard. It's that cold!

There are two parts or reference points of your decision to get out of bed which are important.

The first is the instant you commit to action, that point when you commence physically sneaking back the doona and blankets and sheet so as not to suck in too much uncomfortably cold air before easing yourself over the side of the bed to the vertical and thence to the job of opening the door. (As little and as quickly as possible.)

The second reference point is what you were feeling at the time leading up to and immediately after the commitment point. What layers of emotional wrapping cradled and enclosed the memory information used in committing to the easing-out-of-bed and door-opening?

Were they helpful, easy, positive wrappings or were they nagging, irritating negative wrappings?

You see, what makes the decision to get up and let the cat out a right decision, is how you were set up before the action point and what went on in your critical space immediately afterwards. More precisely, it's how <u>you</u> set <u>yourself</u> up. It's what your Feelings processor, along with your other four mental processors were doing before and after the action point that made getting up either a right or a not-right decision.

"Well, the cat clearly wants to go out. Sleuthing around in the outdoors at night is what cats do. So I'll just let it out ... no questions asked, then back to cozy comfort and dreamy sleep." It was simply just another useful habit you quite happily and deliberately created when you first took in "Mr. Cute" that night in the thunderstorm. You were content in the knowledge that cats are different and this one too, would need your help from time to time, to let him or her be a cat and do what cats have to do.

Or was it like this?

"It's not my cat! It belongs to my sister's grand mother-in-law and we inherited it along with the house when she shifted out of town. It doesn't belong here.

Why should I be the one that has to get up in the freezing cold every time in the middle of the night? Cats were never meant to be pets anyway. They should have been left out in the woods with the tigers and other wild cats. Those Neanderthals or whoever it was who brought them into our houses, have got a lot to answer for. They are the ones who started it all. It's their fault. They are responsible. It's their fault.

It's not fair!"

Or maybe a little more complicated and subtle, like this?

""Haaa!" You thought, not a little guiltily, "If I get up and let the cat out, then I could just sneak by the refrigerator and finish off that wedge of dark, choc sponge left over from desert. It's lying on its side and alone on a plate third shelf up and, if I'm not mistaken, on the far right.""

You know you don't really need it and you know it will probably disagree with you well into tomorrow but what the heck. That satisfying feeling as it goes down your oesophagus will surely lull you back to instant sleep anyway.

In each instance, you decided to get out of bed, and indeed you did just that.

What's different is the emotional wrapping of the deed and the wiring of your five mental energy processors that supported it.

So, which of the three decisions above were right decisions?

Let's look at some of the emotional wrappings and decision ownerships of each case.

In the first instance, there was already a set of values, beliefs and rules about who's responsible for what, including about cats and their place in your world and with which you were quite in agreement.

Your conditioning from family, friends and peers as you were growing set all that up.

You may have consciously tinkered with some parts of your mental wiring and wilfully engaged your Chunks and Bits processor to get more clarity and certainty about the world of you, cats and cold nights however, the call was easy. Even if the house fell down when you opened the door to let "Mr. Cute" out, you would still have owned that decision and taken responsibility for whatever happened, provided, of course, you survived the hypothetical collapse.

Case one ... a right decision.

Case two:

Having to let the cat out became an instant problem and a drain on your energy and mental resources. It caused you pain because your conditioning over time deemed an act such as letting the cat out in such woeful winter circumstances, totally unacceptable. The fact that you did the deed anyway, yet farmed the responsibility (the blame) out to your "not me" world i.e. the Neanderthals and the "nice relative" who left town, was indeed letting the side down ... letting your side down ... letting yourself down. Indeed, it would have to be a case of breaking your own rules about cats, about who aught to do what and how and where. You generated conflicting mental factions for yourself ... what you believed shouldn't have happened opposed to what you actually did in spite of that belief.

And, it may well be truthfully added, what you did, included a measure of significant anger and resentment, two powerful and health-compromising mental energy states.

So, all in all, not a terribly "rightish" decision.

Having said that though, some wilful, constructive afterthought, which acknowledges the "not right-ness" and which commits to conscious improvement, is a stand-alone decision on the "right" side of the decision making equation. It's called <u>constructive self-reflection</u> or <u>positive energy-processor reconstruction</u>, which is great when practised and repeated over and over i.e. it becomes a useful <u>habit of self-correction</u> or <u>self-measurement</u>.

In the third scenario, the dividing line between the "right" and "not right" decision lies between owning and enjoying the pleasure of the extra indulgent snack and the guilt of breaking a diet rule ... of letting your own side down. "I'm weak and am never going to lose weight," is nothing to do with the "rightness" or "not rightness" of deciding to let the cat out.

The warm bed, cat, door and cold night are almost irrelevant. That decision was a mere carrier <u>decision</u>, an excuse, a means to another end, a kind of neutral decision, if such exists.

Broken rules, in this case, equals guilt, which equals pain, with negative emotional wrappings around that particular cat (and maybe all cats), all "scrummy" cake, cold nights, warm beds and refrigerators. It depends on how often the scenario or ones like it are repeated. It could be setting you up for a not-very-healthy, unconscious habit.

Decision three ... probably not quite a "right" one by our standards.

On the other hand, owning the indulgence, enjoying a slice of the decadent, unnecessary chocolate cake could be viewed as more on the up side or on the "right" side of the decision see-saw i.e. if there is ownership and the values, beliefs and the rules you have about your health in the moral world are in general agreement.

You see, a decision is a right decision if the emotional wrappings of the memory you are creating are right. That means there is an associated feeling that supports and empowers and that is useful and generally positive.

Bear in mind that memories you create by doing and thinking can be those of spiritually motivated deeds or of conative or physical actions. **Every deed we have ever carried out and every thought, has an emotional wrapping and the right wrapping is the particular wrapping of ownership.**

The energy of our Feelings Energy processor is that powerful and it applies even when we decide not to take action, to "not do," to not get up in the cold and let the cat out. Deciding to "not do" is still a decision.

We will see later in Part Two how emotional wrappings, when selectively coupled in a conscious way with one or more of the other four mental processor energies, can make for right decisions all the time; a recipe for consistently generating great results.

Before we launch into the dot point section at the end of the chapter, it's important to ask one very important question:

"What are your other mental processors doing to make your decision a right one while your Feelings processor is busy wrapping up the new events and event processing that will be stored in your memory banks?"

Remember, the other processors are: Your Chunks and Bits Energy processor, your I-Will Energy processor, your Physical Energy processor and your Me Energy processor.

Let's take a brief look at each of these in turn.

Your Chunks and Bits Processor, you will recall, collects information like words, facts, thoughts, ideas and memories and arranges them into patterns that are useful.

It makes sense then, for your Chunks and Bits processor to be at its best for right decision making, it needs to be putting forward the right bits of information and putting them forward in the right sequence.

In a practical sense, that means collecting and applying relevant knowledge, resources (including people), plans, blueprints and objectives and arranging them in an intelligent order and format for a great result. Identifying the right equipment to be used with the right materials in the right environment and used in the right way is not really such a big ask for any trained and conscientious professional such as yourself.

It's when those boxes are not ticked, when tools are misused, when not all the necessary information or people are present or the people on the job lack the necessary skills, that a decision can go "pear shaped" and turn into "not right" i.e. into a catastrophe, a disaster, an unfortunate eventuality or just a plain straight forward mess. We will find out in the next few chapters how the risks of these kinds of results can be greatly reduced or eliminated altogether.

When your I-Will processor has to operate outside of its system of needs for how you like to do what you do, or it is overridden by a different set of constraints, e.g. someone else's rules or system, mental tension and strain set in. Mental energy is spent in dealing with this resistance and the action of carrying out the decision becomes laborious, a drag and stressful. It sets up your Feelings processor for what it is designed to do very well, encasing your new decision making experience in all manner of negative, unhealthy, disempowering and draining emotional energy wrappings, all stored away in your conscious and subconscious memory banks for later, upsetting and generally painful retrieval. The resulting inefficient, low-productivity effort generates a "not-so-crash-hot result," another catastrophe or disaster, another outcome that falls way short of the magnificent objective you had in mind when the decision was made at the outset.

Your I-Will Energy processor serves at its peak in a right decision, when you accommodate your wired-in, conative needs one hundred percent for how you operate to do your best work.

Right physical energy processing for right decisions is straight forward. It's simply a matter of asking yourself these two questions:

1. Do I have the physical capability to do the job? That means at the micro-biochemical, autonomic, unconscious level as well as at the big-picture level i.e. the level of physical strength, agility and dexterity and most importantly, your state of physical health and fitness.

2. How much training and physical practice have I done to prepare my body for the decision making exercise? Physical conditioning, through timed repetition, is a number one ingredient for right decision making.

Now, you may want to point out that people with massive physical disabilities can make terrific and consistently right decisions. How come?

Once again, it's all in the emotional wrapping they have put in place around their disabilities. For these people, those wrappings will be of the powerfully positive kind. "I will "nail" this! All I have to do is take a fresh look at what I've got to work with, set a target, make some plans and go for it no matter what."

You have met these inspiring human beings.

So at last, how does your Me Energy processor need to be set up for right decisions?

Whatever you believe about where you came from, why you are on the planet and how you make sense of your universe, must have a presence or be represented or feature in some way whenever you make a decision, even unconscious, habitual ones.

What you believe about divinity, universal intelligence, God or not God, are an integral part of your system of beliefs and must, at the very least, be acknowledged for your decision to qualify as a right one. Without such acknowledgment, your decision grates against an essential and fundamental part of you and is therefore not one hundred percent authentically you nor could you truthfully one hundred percent claim it and own it.

To serve you as an aid to making your decisions right decisions wherever you are, here are five right-decision propositions for your home, office or mental notice board. (There are five extras should you be a more in-depth thinker.)

Ten Propositions for making Right Decisions

1. **Every decision is a choice.**

2. **At their simplest and most basic level, decisions are meanings assigned to sensory and non-sensory events.**

3. **Right decisions are made under the combined influence of the decision maker's mind, body and spiritual self.**

4. **A right decision is made when the decision maker accepts responsibility for and takes ownership of the decision outcome, no matter what.**

5. **To consciously not-decide is a decision in itself and not deciding may sometimes be a right decision.**

6. Conscious and unconscious decisions collectively create an illusion of time passing and of space occupied and therefore an illusion of a sensory and mental world.

7. There is a state in which there can be no decisions because that state is outside of time and space. That state is under the control of the human will and can be entered and exited via a faculty of the will called <u>intent</u>.

8. The human will is in direct contact with a cosmic or universal will and is therefore subject to cosmic decisions. Cosmic decisions are the manifestation of fluctuations in a "universal field of intelligence."

9. The "universal field of intelligence," as far as human beings are concerned, just is ... it must simply be.

10. Reason has no application beyond the "universal field of intelligence." It is simply a tool for decision making, totally within the universal field and manifesting within the illusions of time and space.

On now, to the dot points.

CH 6 FOR THE DOT POINTERS

What Makes a Decision a Right Decision?

- **A right decision is a decision that you own.**

- **In a right decision, the driving force, the outcome and the result of the decision are all a part of you and no other person or organization or universe.**

- **The personal, mental space you call your own is the sum total of every decision you have ever made.**

- **The vehicle on which every one of your decisions rides is either your need to get or make something better or your desire to get away from something causing you pain or grief.**

- There are two vital reference points to every decision you make:

  1) The instant you commit to action

  And

  2) What you were feeling leading up to and immediately after the point of committing to action

- What makes your decisions "right" or "not right" are the emotional wrappings around your <u>intent</u> to act and around the collective operation of your five mental energy processors which prompt and support the action.

- Wilful and constructive afterthought which acknowledges the "not-rightness" of any one of your decisions and which commits to conscious improvement, can become a right decision. With practice, such commitment and repetition can generate the useful habit of self-correction.

- Breaking your rules when you make a decision can equate to guilt. This equals emotional pain and is therefore a negative wrapping around every element of that decision.

- If you completely own the breaking of your rules when you indulge in something you know may not serve you or your world well, then your decision to indulge may be a right one.

- Every decision you have ever made ... every thought ... has an emotional wrapping. The right wrapping is the wrapping of ownership.

- **To make a right decision:**

  <u>Your Chunks and Bits Energy processor</u> must effectively collect mental data on available resources and arrange it intelligently to achieve the best result for the decision.

  <u>Your I Will Energy processor</u> must, one hundred percent, engage your wired-in, conative needs that allow you to do your best work.

  <u>Your Physical Energy processor</u> must have access to an efficient, healthy, physical body so that the new and already-learned skills needed for your decision can be practised and conditioned-in for the best result.

  <u>Your Me Energy processor</u> must acknowledge and build into the decision what you believe about divinity, universal intelligence, God or "Not God."

  <u>Your Feeling Energy processor</u> must wrap every element of your decision in feelings that are positive and which will serve you for that decision and every decision that follows.

Ten Propositions for making Right Decisions

1. *Every decision is a choice.*

2. *At their simplest and most basic level, decisions are meanings assigned to sensory and non-sensory events.*

3. *Right decisions are made under the combined influence of the decision maker's mind, physical body and spiritual self.*

4. *A right decision is made when the decision maker accepts responsibility for and takes ownership of the decision outcome, no matter what.*

5. *To consciously not-decide is a decision in itself and not deciding may sometimes be a right decision.*

Extras for more in-depth consideration:

6. *Conscious and unconscious decisions collectively create an illusion of time passing and of space occupied and therefore an illusion of a sensory and mental world.*

7. *There is a state in which there can be no decisions because that state is outside of time and space. That state is under the control of the human will and can be entered and exited via a faculty of the will called <u>intent</u>.*

8. *The human will is in direct contact with a cosmic or universal will and is therefore subject to cosmic decisions. Cosmic decisions are the manifestation of fluctuations in a "universal field of intelligence."*

9. *The "universal field of intelligence," as far as human beings are concerned, just is ... it must simply be.*

10. *Reason has no application beyond the "universal field of intelligence." It is simply a tool for decision making, totally within the universal field and manifesting within the illusions of time and space.*

CHAPTER 7

OLD MESS OR NEW MEANING

CHAPTER 7

OLD MESS OR NEW MEANING?

(Giving the "mess in your head" a new meaning to find out what needs fixing.)

So, what does need working on?

What's not happening for you right now?

What's "bugging" you?

What's driving you from one distraction to another?

What's making you throw up your hands in dismay because it's all a bit too much?

How much "poor me" have you been doing lately?

Before we go there though, we must back-track a little and ask a question, a course-correcting question.

Given that you've read Part One (or some of it) and the previous couple of pages, you may want to ask yourself, "Have I got what I'm looking for from the read so far or am I still in and ready to surge forwards, to keep playing on for more of the "what's-in-it-for-me?"

If so, play on. Skip the next paragraph and surge forwards.

If you decided it's enough for the time being and you're happy with your new-found knowledge and direction gleaned from Part One, that's okay. Before you put the book down though, please do take one more, small step. Please flick to the last chapter. It's your part of the work to take with you or to leave as you see fit.

Thank you for making the effort to choose this book and for making the time to read this far. May your five great mental energy processors serve you well towards making your every decision a right decision.

So, what's not working for you right now?

If you've ever been a "first-aider" or know a nurse or doctor or maybe you're a loving, caring parent who manages your children's knocks and bumps as they grow and learn, the first step in helping someone in need or in pain is to check for tell-tale signs or symptoms of known conditions. This is a very important information-gathering first step.

Next, you flick through the first aid knowledge stored neatly in your memory banks for such an occasion and follow up with the appropriate response drill stored there under the label "First Aid Training and Experience."

E.g. Is there redness or swelling around the knee joint of your distraught and unhappy two-year-old or of your mate's elbow after he dived for a catch in a game of beach cricket at Christmas? Is there any bleeding?

Is the limb moving normally?

Some cool clean water, a small bandage and some positive words may be all that's needed and all's well.

Sometimes it's not that straight-forward. Symptoms aren't always as obvious or as graphic as a major, physical catastrophe.

Headaches, feeling sick, back pain that lingers are symptoms too and signs that something's amiss or not quite right inside or outside, or maybe both however, there isn't a lot of clear evidence to work with and not many clues you can see or touch or listen for. Bandages, soothing words and water probably aren't going to be enough either. More information is needed, so you head off to the nurse or doctor or specialist, depending on the situation and how your decision making blueprint as the first aider or carer or responsible person is set up.

So much for first aid on the physical.

What's the first aid for our <u>non-physical bodies,</u> for that inner mind-space where equally vital non-physical processes are happening all the time? What's the first aid when that part of you gets hurt or "out of whack?"

It's the same deal as for the beach cricket ... look for signs that something's amiss and symptoms of known conditions that can be clearly identified and on which you can focus.

So, what are these signs or symptoms? **What do you need to look for in order to do non-physical, mind first aid?**

Have you ever felt down, depressed, scared, anxious or lonely or sad or angry?

You would go for a "yes," as would just about every other human being on the planet. Every one of those "not-happy" feelings is a sign or symptom that something's not right and needs attention. Often it's no big deal. The episode blows over and you are "back in the game" like the clean water, bandage and words of comfort on the playing field or the beach.

The question we must ask is, "How often are those feelings coming around?"

Are they frequent visitors?

Are they hanging around all the time and refusing to go away, as if they were being worn like some clingy, uncomfortable overcoat or like cobwebs and accumulated off-cuts and filings and sawdust in the workshop or like overflowing tidy bins and empty tubes and tubs of this and that on the dressing room vanity unit?

If your answer is, "Yes," "A lot," "All the time," "It never goes away" or "The world always has it in for me," then something is amiss and it is time to take action ... right now. Using the E.C.R.O.M. idea, you have simply collected a "head-full" of registered events in your Critical Space, some of which are useful and some which are not so. Choosing to ignore them or pretending they aren't there, may lead to a mental "breakage" soon.

In the chapters that follow, you will discover how applying what you already know about the E.C.R.O.M. idea can convert what at first appears to be a stressful, seemingly impossible mental and physical mess, into an opportunity to simply change some meanings about what you are experiencing.

You will also discover how to step back from yourself and realign your five mental energy processors so that they are in sync with one another and "churning out" right decisions for you every time.

Check out the dot points and then read on to find out how to convert an impossible looking mess into a new and empowering opportunity that will serve you better.

CH 7 FOR THE DOT POINTERS

Old Mess or New Meaning?

- **The first step in helping someone in need or in pain is to check for tell-tale signs or symptoms of any known conditions.**

- **Next, recall the necessary first-aid knowledge and follow up with the appropriate first-aid response drill.**

- **Symptoms aren't always as obvious or as graphic as in a major physical catastrophe.**

- Headaches, feeling sick, back pain that lingers are signs that something in your physical body is amiss. First aid skills may not be enough and help from the medical professionals may be needed.

- First aid for your non-physical body follows the same game-plan. Look for mental signs and symptoms such as feeling "down," depressed, scared, anxious, sad or angry.

- Ask how often those feelings are coming up and check in with a professional.

- Choosing to ignore or deny the symptoms that exist may lead to a mental "breakage"

- In the following chapters, you will discover how to use what appears to be a mental or physical "mess" as an opportunity to change the meaning of what you are experiencing.

- You will also discover how to realign your five mental energy processors so that they are in sync and how to make every decision a right decision.

CHAPTER 8

RECONDITIONING YOUR DECISION-MAKING MACHINERY

CHAPTER 8

RECONDITIONING YOUR DECISION-MAKING MACHINERY

Remember that whatever the decision, whether a micro-neuro-molecular or a mega, life-and-death decision, your mental energy processors are all engaged. Though it may appear that only one or two are active, all five of them are at work.

This next important section is on overhauling or reconditioning your decision making machinery.

To overhaul anything ... the engine in your car, your staff management practices, your wardrobe, your current domestic budgeting system or your old mountain bike, you need to understand its current condition or state of play.

As we are focusing on your decision making machinery, it makes sense to take each component of your mental energy processing machine in turn and find out what it's doing as you are making your hundreds and thousands and tens of thousands and millions of decisions. Under this "reconditioning" banner, you will discover how your mental energy workshops or dressing rooms <u>could </u>work i.e. what they could achieve, if they were allowed to do what they were set up to do without interference from each other. To understand how each of our mental workshops is constructed, we need to know how it is designed and how it actually works individually.

That may seem a bit artificial however, it's no different from the whole E.C.R.O.M. idea anyway. It's a useful idea and a tool to help understand something that we can't actually see, hear, touch, taste or smell.

We must put our whole decision making process under the microscope, find out how each component works and then apply what we discover to our own decision making world.

Remember, in the E.C.R.O.M. model for decision making, "C" represents your Critical Space and your Critical Space houses your five mental energy processors: Chunks and Bits (Cognitive), Feelings (Affective), I-Will (Conative), Physical (Psychomotor) and Me (Spiritual).

Sometimes, a great way to understand a piece of equipment or a system is to examine what happens when it's <u>not</u> working at its best.

We will use this approach on each part of your decision making process in turn as a lead-up to finding out how to improve their individual and collective performances.

To do justice to this investigation, considerably more detail than can comfortably be included in this book will be needed. It's a bit like checking each moving part of a car gear box or testing each electronic component of a theatre sound mixer. There is an enormous and intricate assortment of parts and connections, each one vital for the successful function of the unit. With this in mind as you read on, get ready in the next chapter, to download our newly-developed and complimentary, companion e-book: *"Reconditioning Your Critical Space. What Happens When Your Decision Making Energy Works Against You and What To Do About It."* (Or you can download it right now at: <u>www.howtomaketherightdecisioneverytime.com</u>.)

CH 8 FOR THE DOT POINTERS

Overhauling Your Decision Making Machinery

- **Whenever you make a decision, all five of your mental energy processors are engaged.**

- **To overhaul your decision making machinery, you need to understand the current state of play in each of its working parts.**

- **One way to discover the current state of play in any system is to examine what happens when it's under-performing.**

8.1 GIVING YOUR EVENT REGISTRATION MACHINERY A WORK-OVER

Remember that events are simply changes that happen in your outside world and inside your physical body and mental space.

Remember also that we are aware of change mainly because we have a memory.

No memory means we would have no "yardsticks" or benchmarks against which to compare what's happening right now.

Out of all the billions of changes going on in the outside world, only some are registered in our Critical Space. These are the <u>events</u> we have deemed useful to us at the time. The remainder becomes background "noise" and, as far as we know, doesn't figure much in our internal physical and mental processing.

Some of the incoming event registration is automatic because it happens over and over. Such recurrence of an event makes this registration a <u>habit</u> ... usually an unconscious one.

Knowing you have to stop at red traffic lights, recognising familiar words when we read, such as the, but, and, on and or, and recognising objects we see all the time like trees, clouds, houses and people are all evidence of habitual, event registration.

We have learned these habits because these events are repeatedly useful to us. Some events are life-and-death events and registering them fast and unconsciously is a survival mechanism e.g. events like feeling the land fall away beneath you at the edge of a cliff or hearing and seeing a boulder tumbling towards you down a hillside.

The common factor in all of these events that are registered in your Critical Space is that they are "attracted" by your needs and desires, the need to escape and survive, the need to avoid pain and the desire to find or achieve something you want.

How can we make sure that those events that are registered always <u>serve</u> us and do not stand in our way?

How can we make sure that, out of all the billions of events happening outside and inside our body, we only attract the ones that will keep us alive, that will keep us healthy and keep us making right decisions?

The secret to attracting the right events for registration lies in our wants and desires.

We must make sure that these two critical driving forces in our lives are wholesome, life-supporting and positive all the time.

Deciding to stay alive, deciding to be healthy and deciding to be prosperous, will attract the events needed to satisfy those desires.

Questions are powerful magnets for attracting the right events and one of the best questions to ask ourselves above all others is the "How-can-I?" question.

How can I stay alive?

How can I stay healthy?

How can I be even more prosperous?

How can I be of more service?

When such questions are asked, your subconscious activates your Reticular Activating System (RAS) which is that part of your brain that draws your attention, for example, to all of the cars the same make and model and colour as the new one you just bought or every other woman wearing the same dress as the one you bought and thought was the one-and-only in town.

After asking this question, it's just a matter of being aware and alert for the answers and opportunities to take the necessary action to achieve what you want.

When asking the "How-do-I?" question is practised and becomes ingrained in your daily life as a habit, the natural laws of manifestation and attraction are enacted automatically and you experience your life as an effortless "flow."

Whatever it is you seek, turns up.

Whatever it is you need, manifests.

Opportunities to move closer to your desired objective that answer your "How-can-I?" question appear sometimes quite "out of the blue." It seems you didn't engineer them yourself however, you are certainly grateful they came your way.

When this happens on a consistent basis, your world becomes a breeze, an even more wonderful and happy place to be.

"Right" event registration just does that.

Before the dot points, there is one addition to the "How-can-I?" question, and it's a clincher.

Your life will become an astoundingly beautiful one when asking yourself this "How-can-I?" question becomes a habit:

"How can I use this event in my life for the highest good?"

Of course, you can make up your own "How-can-I-highest-good" questions as you see fit. Your sub-conscious and mental energy processors will still work their magic.

Now for your mind-behind-the-mind summary.

CH 8.1 FOR THE DOT POINTERS

Giving your Event Registration a Work-over

- **Events are simply changes that happen in your outside world and in your inside physical and mental space.**

- **Your memory provides yardsticks and reference points against which to compare what's happening in your life right now.**

- **Only changes that you deem useful at the time are registered in your Critical Space.**

- When the same event is registered over and over as repeatedly useful to you, registration of that event becomes an unconscious habit e.g. recognising common objects and words.

- The common factor in all of the events that are registered in your Critical Space is that they are attracted by your needs and desires.

- Ensuring that your desires are wholesome, life-supporting and positive all the time, sets you up for a life of right decisions.

- "How can I?" questions are powerful magnets for attracting right events into your life e.g. "How can I lose more weight?"

- Such questions activate your Reticular Activating System (RAS) which draws your attention to useful events from that time onwards.

- When asking "How-can-I?" questions becomes a habit, the natural laws of manifestation and attraction are automatically enacted.

- Events that are attracted by your "How-can-I?" question can sometimes turn up unexpectedly i.e. you didn't plan for them.

- The most powerful "How-can-I?" question you can ask yourself is, "How can I use this event in my life for the highest good?"

8.2 RECONDITIONING YOUR CRITICAL SPACE

And now, as a dive into the real mental nitty gritty, let's "home in on" that great crucible and cradle of your world, your decision making foundry and nursery, that which makes you think what you think and do what you do, your Critical Space.

Remember, your Critical Space is the mental zone between an event happening in your life and the action you take (or don't take) as a result. The event can either be an internal mind event or a physical one in your outside world. Your Critical Space also houses your five great (or sometimes, not-so-great) mental energy processors: Chunks and Bits, Feelings, I Will, Physical and Me Energy.

What happens when these powerful and vital movers and shakers are off beat, "out of whack" or simply not serving you?

How do you know, for example, when your Chunks and Bits processor is letting you down, struggling with too much uncertainty ... letting Feelings energy onto its normally pristine playing field of logic and reason?

And what about your Feelings processor?

Is it delivering pain overload and setting you up with habits you know you so desperately want to throw overboard? Has it set you up with conflicting values where you often seem to find yourself between the proverbial rock and a hard place?

Does your I Will processor keep you operating in your "sweet spot" where everything is a breeze? What happens when it isn't and things aren't going swimmingly? **What happens when tasks take forever and use up so much of your precious mental and physical energy even though you know you've done your best** and having to work with certain people keeps you in a relentlessly stressful state? Maybe you are forced to work in ways you know aren't right for you and make you feel so drained that all you want to do is just quit. Your I Will processor may be in need of some TLC (tender loving care).

Are you feeding your Physical Energy processor "clean" energy to work with? Clean energy means physically uncontaminated (food, air and water) and in a positive mental state.

Everyone has mind chatter. How do you know when your internal conversations are blotting out your unique "you-ness" i.e. when your Me processor seems to have "dropped off the radar," when you're not taking much notice of where you fit in with what's going on around you and your life seems to be just one mindless reaction after another.

There are so many questions and so many answers hidden away in an apparently jumbled mental matrix of certainty and uncertainty, pleasure, pain frustration and satisfaction.

Questions however, can be one of the most powerful forces for positive change.

A great teacher once said, "The answer is inherent in the question."

May I suggest your answers to such questions already exist, harboured within your ever-industrious, mental, decision making workshop ... your very own Critical Space.

All that's needed is a rigorous teasing out of this apparent jumble of question-energy threads, sorting them and then reinstating those sensational mental states of clarity, order and focus you know you enjoyed way back before everything changed.

To help with the teasing out, the order, the clarity and the focus, we have created for you a tailor-made, right-decision, answer-finding guide to help and support you as you step inside your Critical Space workshop for its eminent clean-out and refurbishment. It is called: *"Reconditioning Your Critical Space. What Happens When Your Decision Making Energy Works Against You and What To Do About It."* This faithful, right-decision guide, designed to be your right-hand-person and loyal, Critical Space companion throughout the process is a simple, yet comprehensively structured e-book. It will ease you through an investigation of your Critical Space mental energy workshop and into a reconditioning action plan. You can download it right now, for <u>free,</u> at: <u>www.howtomaketherightdecisioneverytime.com</u>.

In this companion guide, you will find much more detailed explanations of how your mental energy processors function than could possible fit into this book and what to look for when they are under-performing. What it is not, however, is an authoritative reference on how to treat mental illness. It is simply an aid to trouble-shooting your Critical mind-space using the E.C.R.O.M. idea for making right decisions.

Happy investigation, trouble-shooting and reconditioning!

And now for a Critical Space, reconditioning, dot point overview.

CH 8.2 FOR THE DOT POINTERS

Reconditioning Your Critical Space

- **Your Critical Space is the mental zone between an event happening in your life and the action you take (or don't take) as a result.**

- **Your Critical Space also houses your five great (or sometimes, not-so-great) mental energy processors: Chunks and Bits, Feelings, I Will, Physical and Me Energy.**

- **Reconditioning your Critical Space energy processors means asking questions, sometimes the hard questions, about what's not working for you.**

- **To find the answers, all that's needed is a clear commitment to do so.**

- *"Reconditioning Your Critical Space. What Happens When Your Decision Making Energy Works Against You and What To Do About It"* is your e-book companion, especially designed to guide and support you in critically exploring and refurbishing your Critical Space. You can downloaded it right now at: www.howtomaketherightdecisioneverytime.com

CHAPTER 9

REACTION AND RESPONSE QUALITY CONTROL

CHAPTER 9

REACTION AND RESPONSE QUALITY CONTROL

In Part One of this book, we saw how your reactions and responses to events are set up i.e. what it is in your mental energy space that makes them happen. **Together, your reactions and responses create your conscious and unconscious behaviour.**

We also learned the difference between a reaction and a response and how an informed response can be turned into a reaction as a <u>conditioned habit</u>.

Making sure these two modes of behaviour are serving you and not getting in the way or slowing you down is the subject of this "Quality-Control" chapter.

Once your Critical Space processors have set you up to react or respond, it's important to know how you can check on the <u>quality</u> of your habits of reaction and behavioural responses.

Remember that reactions and responses aren't all physical actions carried out in your physical world. They are also internal, like the automatic feedback systems that control your heartbeat and breathing and the mental activities of thinking and feeling.

Every bit, piece, slice or tiny "morsel" of your behaviour, conscious or unconscious, physical or mental, is either a reaction or a response.

There are countless bits, pieces, slices and "morsels" of behaviour going on every moment of your life and it makes sense that you could never do a quality check on every single one of them.

What you must do in order to guarantee the best outcome, the best result, and ultimately a right decision, is focus on those behaviours that are important at the time i.e. the reactions and responses relevant to the current decision being made.

Given that your five mental energy processors have been overhauled and tuned up to peak efficiency, all that is needed is a way of monitoring these "relevant" reactions and responses.

Internal, neurochemical reactions like heartbeat, hormone release and white blood cell production can only be monitored indirectly by focussing on the measurable signs and symptoms of such activity.

Being aware of signs and symptoms and comparing them against a standard or what we believe is normal is the first step.

The second step is deciding whether to act or not act, when the signs and symptoms are above or below this benchmark.

Being aware of your racing heart and rapid breathing when there appears to be no apparent reason is an example of such reaction monitoring.

Monitoring your less obvious conscious thoughts and physical actions requires skills that can be learned and practiced.

These are mostly skills of <u>self-observation,</u> <u>introspection</u> or <u>self-reflection</u>.

A useful way to explain how to "watch" yourself is to imagine you are in a movie theatre and an engaging action movie is playing on the big screen.

"Engagement" means that you are drawn right into and become a part of the story, feeling the emotion, weathering the traumas and celebrating the triumphs of the characters. You are right there, alongside the hero and heroine. It's an exhilarating, exciting place to be.

The movie ends and it takes a while for your heart rate to settle down and your excitement to subside. You return to your reality in the street outside and the movie, over time, becomes a memory of an exciting and entertaining fantasy.

For some people, return to everyday life is not quite complete. The emotions and sensations of the fantasy become lodged in their conscious and subconscious memories, stored alongside the facts and figures, the beliefs and rules they use in their everyday lives.

Keeping such unhelpful fiction out of your memory banks is where self-observation comes into its own. Blocking those incoming fantasies before they manage to slip through your registration "filters" allows the events that serve you clearer passage into your mental processing and storage spaces.

Attracting into your mental space only those events that will serve you is a must.

Imagine now, a different kind of movie, one where you aren't drawn in and where you are more <u>emotionally passive</u> and mostly <u>observing</u> the story, instead of being up there in the action with the leads. You are monitoring their decisions, their emotions, their deeds and their motives. Your engagement is in assessing, evaluating, judging and critiquing what you are witnessing.

It's as if there's an invisible barrier between you sitting there in the auditorium and the action on the screen.

At the end of the movie, your head is full of comments you want to make, questions you want to ask and opinions you are keen to share with others willing to compare notes.

A third film scenario is where you are the screen writer for the film as well as the director.

The screen writer creates the story. The director selects the cast of actors whose talents and movements he directs to create the film version of the story.

As writer-director, you convert the intangible mental "cloud" of plot, story line, character personalities, history and setting into a visual experience for the fans and share it with the world.

When you monitor your behaviour to keep tabs on your reactions and responses, it's like the second movie scenario above where you watch yourself objectively, just as you watched the characters of the movie without attachment. Watching yourself without being affected by your emotions and actions and the stories playing out in your head, is like enjoying a birds-eye view of yourself. It's a bit like what a Martian would observe as "it" secretly watched you live out your life on planet earth.

Viewing your world of reactions and responses from these three different "film" perspectives or vantage points, is the same as experiencing your world from three different Me Energy processor vantage points which, you will recall, are the different mental states within your Me Energy processor for processing incoming information.

What is worth exploring right now, is viewing your behaviour using this third movie scenario i.e. being a conscious creator of your world, writing your own life script and directing your life, adding in the emotions you would like to experience and engineering the outcome of your every decision.

Professional athletes, sports people, dancers, business people and great leaders use this technique of self-monitoring and directing all the time. Such people are constantly watching themselves, alert to diversions from the path they want to follow and always giving themselves objective, detached feedback on what they observe. Monitoring your behaviour in this way will set you up for a right decision every time.

Monitoring your behaviour on a more hands-on or practical level, is easy. Recording your behaviour by keeping a diary, video filming your performance or audio taping what you say are easy ways to give you valuable feedback on "you." It's not just for the athletes, dancers and great public speakers, you can do it too.

Writing down your thoughts, observations and reflections on your performance is a great way to develop a habit of self-monitoring. Some people call it journaling or simply keeping a "thought diary." *"Transformations. A Guided Journal"* by Zoe-Anne Fields is a great book to help with just that.

Throwing away what you've written or videoed or recorded is okay. It's a record of you, for you and nobody else. The observations and feedback have been done and the plusses and items for improvement have been consciously noted.

With practice, monitoring your behaviour and giving yourself feedback on your progress to where you want to be or what you want to achieve, can become continuous and turn into a useful habit, at your disposal, any time you want.

Right decisions require conscious monitoring of your reactions and responses. Right decisions also require your constructive feedback on what you observe about yourself all the time.

And now for the twelve hot, dot points for keeping your eye on you.

CH 9 FOR THE DOT POINTERS

Reaction and Response Quality Control

- **Together, your reactions and responses create your conscious and unconscious behaviour.**

- **With commitment and practice, a conscious, informed response can be turned into a useful, unconscious habit.**

- **Reactions and responses are invisible, internal, automatic, feedback behaviours as well as observable, physical actions.**

- **Invisible, internal, neurochemical reactions like your heartbeat, hormone release and white blood cell production can only be monitored indirectly by consciously observing signs and symptoms of such activity.**

- External, physical action and conscious thoughts can be monitored directly by engaging skills of self-observation and self-reflection (introspection).

- There are three ways to experience your own behaviour:

    - Being totally engaged in the action with little or no critical thought

    - Observing your behaviour with a detached and unbiased mindset

    - As a creator and deliberate manager of your behaviour

- Some people become so "mindlessly" engaged in the action and fantasies of their lives, that "pieces" of fantasy get mixed up and confused with their everyday working beliefs, rules, facts and figures.

- Removing these fantasies and blocking their entry into your mental space allows a greater attraction of events that will serve you.

- Watching yourself in a detached way is the same as experiencing a bird's-eye view of your behaviour.

- Whenever you witness or observe or consciously create and manage your reactions and responses in a detached way, you are viewing your world from different I-Will processor vantage points.

- **Top athletes, performers and great leaders constantly watch themselves and give themselves valuable, objective and detached feedback on their performance.**

- **Recording your behaviour via writing, video or sound recording are easy and practical ways of developing the useful habit of self-monitoring.**

CHAPTER 10

GETTING THE OUTCOME YOU WANT

CHAPTER 10

GETTING THE OUTCOME YOU WANT

Whether it's a journey, creating a piece of art work, repairing a broken chair, removing old nail polish or refurbishing your worn-out kitchen, **every wilful, conscious, human endeavour or project is carried out twice.**

The project happens first in your mind-space and then on the physical plane as you arrive at your destination or make, repair, refurbish or remove whatever it is you had in mind. When you want or desire something, you create it first in your mental space. This happens as an idea or thought about why you want whatever it is you want, what exactly it is and how you will achieve the objective. You then take some action by reacting or responding (or both), to the idea. What you want eventually becomes physical and real, provided that is, you are committed and stick with the task.

Creating the idea or <u>initial mental outcome</u> happens in your Critical Space as a response or reaction to something that's happened either as an event in your external world or a memory event in your mind-space. Knowing how to increase the chances of this idea or initial mental outcome coming to fruition or manifesting, is mostly the work of your Chunks and Bits mental energy processor.

Remember that this processor works with facts, with knowledge of the laws, rules, principles and protocols you decide are essential to the outcome you are first creating in your mind. Your Chunks and Bits processor will use the mental <u>skills</u> required to move this knowledge around in your Critical Space workshops and then apply it to <u>analyse</u> for relevance and suitability. It's a sort of mental editing of your plan.

Finally, your Chunks and Bits processor will engage your powers of mental <u>synthesis</u> to create a clear picture in your mind's eye of what your objective will look like when it's finished. This mental picture could be a combination of smells, tastes, sounds and physical texture as well as visuals.

Knowing that your own <u>beliefs</u> and <u>values</u> are going to play a role in formulating the initial mental outcome is vital. **Your values and beliefs can be great supporters or great blockers to coming up with an outcome and plan to achieve it, that's going to work for you.**

Remember that your beliefs and rules come with an emotional component and they are powerful drivers in creating both the initial mental outcome and the emotion needed for the final physical version of it to take shape. **Every desire or want has an outcome with an emotion at its core.**

Remember also that every memory you have in your conscious and subconscious memory banks has some emotion attached as an emotional wrapping. Positive, empowering, emotional wrappings are a must for assembling a true and clear initial-outcome idea.

Your I-Will processor will also be nudging you towards a plan that allows you to operate from your conative "sweet spot," from that mental space that allows you easy and efficient use of your mental and physical energy to solve problems in the way that you know suits you best. Your Chunks and Bits helps out too when it comes to working with that same, wired-in need in others involved in helping you achieve your objective.

Sound and effective planning in creating a clear idea of your desired outcome from the start has three requirements: A clean supply of energy for your mental energy processors to do what they are designed to do, intake of clean air and intake of clean water. Your Physical Energy processor must have these three vital supplies for efficient energy use with your other mental energy workshops. Your Me processor is set up to provide you with different Me Energy vantage points through which to view your initial mental objective. If you were to view your objective from one point only, the chances of blocks, barriers and derailments in the implementation phase are likely to increase. View your objective idea from as many different Me Energy vantage points as you can. Remember the cinema story from the previous chapter: Are you inside the action of your planning? Are you viewing it critically and detached from your seat in the auditorium? Are you operating the projection equipment or are you writing and directing the whole operation yourself?

Make sure the following six boxes are ticked when your mental objective appears complete and before you start getting your idea up and running:

1. Know precisely why you want or desire whatever it is you want or desire. At the end of every one of your desires and wants is a particular emotional state. Maybe it's a feeling of satisfaction on winning the race or feeling peaceful and connected after a happy family reunion or exhilaration on reaching the top of the mountain or safe landing after a skydive with free-fall from four thousand metres.

2. Know precisely <u>what</u> it is that you want to experience when your initial mental objective eventually becomes a reality. What will your senses be telling you? What will the sounds, smells and tastes be like? Paint a clear picture in your mind's eye of what you want in as much detail as you possibly can.

3. Know <u>how</u> you will get to your destination, how you will create the object, artwork, story or system you want to create.

4. Know <u>when</u> it will happen. Set time markers along your project journey. Remember, you can always modify and adapt along the way using your measuring-on-the-run skills.

5. Cover as many <u>what-if</u> bases as you can. These are called contingency plans and they allow you to efficiently deal with unforeseen and potentially derailing eventualities.

6. Finally, **know and believe, with absolute certainty, that your initial mental objective is achievable. It will happen!**

Now, it's time for the action, the implementation or execution phase, to convert your initial mental objective into a culminating reality you can experience.

Remember, right **results come from attracting right events from your outside environment and your inner mind-space.** You must constantly monitor both your internal and external behaviours and be ready to self-correct as you carry out your plan. Self-monitoring increases the chance of identifying distractions and diversions <u>before</u> they take you off course or derail your project.

Be aware of those factors relevant to your objective that you know you <u>can</u> control and those you know you can't. In the implementation stage, know that some factors and forces you <u>can't</u> control are the very ones working for you when your Me processor is at work. Allow those factors a place in the implementation of your plan by viewing your behaviour from as many different spiritual energy windows as you can. Factors you can't control can work <u>for</u> you as well as against you.

Those forces over which you believe you have no control can be the greatest barrier-busters you have in your decision making tool box.

The next important point in your execution is knowing <u>when</u> you've reached your objective, for example, identifying exactly when your newly-created system of home finance management starts to work out for you.

If the "what" phase of your initial mental objective was clear and precise in the first place, knowing you've arrived, that you have the prize and that your mission is accomplished, will be obvious. You will know when you have achieved your objective.

Sometimes however, the implementation or execution of your plan may take a few unexpected twists and turns, enough to where your desired outcome may not look, sound, feel, taste or smell exactly as you originally planned. Nevertheless, the new invention works, albeit a little shakily. The artwork or sculpture still holds the magic you saw in your mind's eye at the start and the view from the top of the mountain was spectacular even though it was for only a few fleeting seconds before the mist closed around you.

To conclude this chapter on getting the right outcome, there is one further and very, very important box to be ticked at journey's end.

After you've done the hard yards of blocker-busting, after you've worked your "you" magic, you must make sure your achievement will continue to serve you well. Your achievement must be set up for easy recall, embedded in your subconscious in bright, colourful, jubilant, satisfying emotions. Your newly-manifested objective must become a positive and useful addition to the foundation of all future objectives. Congratulate yourself on a fine achievement. Give yourself a pat on the back for a job well done. Celebrating your successful outcome is the single, biggest "must" of right decision making. Success breeds success.

Let's get down to dot point Earth on the outcome you want.

CH 10 FOR THE DOT POINTERS

Getting the Outcome You Want

- **Every wilful, conscious endeavour is carried out twice, first in your mind-space and then on the physical plane as a physical manifestation.**

- Creating your initial idea happens in your Critical Space in response to or as a reaction to an event in your physical world or inner mind space.

- Determining how to make the idea happen is mostly the work of your Chunks and Bits processor.

- Your beliefs and values play an important role in formulating the idea or initial mental outcome.

- Your I-Will processor prompts you to operate in the way that you know suits you best.

- Your Physical Energy processor must have "clean" energy from right food and clean air and water in order to service and work in with your other mental energy processors.

- View your initial mental objective from as many Me Energy vantage points as you can to see how well it will fit into your world.

- Know precisely <u>why</u> you want or desire this outcome.

- Know <u>what</u> your final outcome will look like in detail. A vague initial mental outcome will produce a vague final outcome.

- Know <u>how</u> you will achieve your outcome. If you can't come up with all the steps, make allowance for the uncertainty.

- Know <u>when</u> it will happen.

- Cover as many contingencies as you can at the start.

- Know what you can and can't control.

- Know when you've reached your outcome.

- Make sure the memory of your achievement is wrapped in strong positive emotions. Congratulate yourself and celebrate.

CHAPTER 11
STAYING ON TRACK WITH RIGHT MEASUREMENT

CHAPTER 11

STAYING ON TRACK WITH RIGHT MEASUREMENT

Remember, with the E.C.R.O.M. idea, measurement is comparing the outcome you get in a decision you made with the outcome you visualised at the start of your decision making process.

Right measurement is where measurement is applied to self-monitor and self-correct as you work physically and mentally towards your objective. It is also setting you up with a useful springboard "event" for your next decision.

Right measurement is also a conscious and wilful process that can be turned into a powerful and useful unconscious habit. All that's needed is commitment and regular practice.

When your desired outcome at the start is clear, with your mental energy processors also clear of obstruction and free to operate as they are naturally designed and allowed to work in sync, right (and useful) measurement can be made when you reach your final outcome.

Right Outcome + Right Measurement = Right Result

That's the big picture. What does right measurement look like in practical terms?

How does it <u>feel</u> to measure what you get with what you wanted or desired at the start?

Let's say you decide to make a new outfit for yourself or build a new workbench (if you're not into sewing).

You made that decision because of an event that was registered as significant, important or useful (or all three) in your Critical Space.

The significance or importance or usefulness gave you a reason or "Why" to make the outfit or the workbench.

You may have agreed to be a bridesmaid at your best friend's wedding and certainly want that outfit to match the occasion in splendid fashion.

The workbench is a must because you've just set yourself up as a sole trader in small steel fabrication and design. That bench is going to be a number-one workhorse for generating your income, at least for the next five years.

Remember from the previous chapter, your initial mental objective or outcome must be crystal clear for the best result and there are two "musts" for initial outcome clarity:

1. You must identify the <u>feeling</u> you want from your outcome at the end of the project. Your bridesmaid's dress, when you wear it at the wedding, must make you feel totally <u>happy</u> and <u>satisfied</u> that you look your very best. Your best friend deserves that, as does every single one of the wedding guests. The workbench must guarantee you the <u>certainty</u> and <u>peace of mind</u> that it will allow you to perform the many different tasks you know you will have to perform as a steel fabricator and designer.

Right bridesmaid's outfit = Happy and satisfied.

Right workbench = Certainty and peace of mind.

2. Create in your mind's eye what your outfit or workbench will <u>look like</u>, down to the smallest significant detail. Your mind's-eye view must be of your product in action, not just when you've finished making it. What working features must the workbench or bridesmaid's dress have for you to experience the happiness and satisfaction, the certainty and peace of mind?

    Of course, if you were a composer creating a new work, it would be your mind's "ear" that gives you initial clarity on how the finished work will sound or your mind's "nose" or "taste buds" if you were a creative chef working up a new banquet dish.

In meeting these two conditions, you are creating a clear and sound reference point or benchmark against which to measure your final working outcome. This <u>primary measurement</u> or comparison will create your <u>primary result</u> ... the ultimate verdict on the success of your bridesmaid's dress or amazing workbench.

Questions will unavoidably come up:

"Was I truly happy and satisfied on the wedding day beside my best friend and her groom and in front of all those guests or am I kidding myself?"

"Did I feel safe and confident that the bench did what I wanted it to do? Is it going to work for all the other jobs that are likely to come up over the next five years?"

It is in the next stage of your bridesmaid's outfit or workbench decision that your skills of <u>secondary measurement</u> are vital.

Secondary measurement relates to the "How" part of your initial mental outcome, your plan of application or execution, and <u>how</u> you are going to produce the dress or workbench or piece of music or banquet dish.

This also means measuring "on the run" i.e. monitoring and mini-correcting the performance of each of your mental energy processors throughout the execution of the project.

As with primary measurement, secondary measurement must have clear and sound reference points in your initial mental objective against which to compare your mini outcomes along the way. It's the "staying-on-track" part of your decision.

Clear and precise detailing of every important component of your initial mental objective is an absolute must. This means a detailed check-list of desired features and functions from the very beginning. Each of your five mental energy processors needs this to set you up for the best result.

The bridesmaid's outfit and the workbench are important, so it makes sense to get the action plan (the "How") right from the start. Your Chunks and Bits processor is going to need some <u>knowledge</u> which you may or may not already have and mental and physical <u>skills</u> to effectively carry out the work e.g. knowledge and skills in drawing or selecting patterns and plans and very likely some basic mathematics and literacy skills. Your Chunks and Bits will also need to <u>analyse</u> the plan or pattern information before cutting the fabric for the dress or the steel for the bench frame.

Should you want some modifications not included in the standard pattern or plan, your Chunks and Bits processor will have to engage its <u>evaluation</u> and <u>synthesis</u> capabilities. In this case, you will most certainly need to self-monitor and adjust as you progress through each stage of your "How-to" plan.

You may even need to learn and practise some new <u>physical</u> skills, especially if it's your first bridal outfit or commercial workbench e.g. pinning the pattern to the fabric so that when the dress is worn, it hangs correctly or keeping the bench legs square as you weld them into their permanent position.

Completing each stage of your project represents a mini-result within the greater decision.

So what happens when your mini-results along the way go "pear-shaped" e.g. you didn't allow enough for the seam here or you cut one steel leg brace half a millimetre short? You will need to adjust and modify your next step and possibly the next and the next and the next, to get your execution phase back on track

Even if the "pear-shape" isn't small, if it's a catastrophic "pear-shape" for instance, you will still have to make a monitoring-on-the-run decision, based on the nature of this mega, on-the-run "pear-shaped" result.

"What can I salvage?"

"Do I need to start again?"

"Can someone help me out of this mess?"

"How can I view this mess in a constructive way?"

Remember too, that final outcomes aren't all physical objects nor are they physical destinations like mountain tops or rock concerts.

Final outcomes can be particular mindsets, like keeping calm in noisy environments or mental skills like adding, subtracting, multiplying or dividing or unconscious mental habits like thinking "smoothie" when you get hungry instead of "cake."

The need for clarity around your initial mental objective and the need for measurement and self-correction "on the run" still applies.

Mindsets or mind states, like being able to maintain a state of serenity, calmness and clarity in a boisterous and violent environment, is a mental state learned and practised and honed and refined, for example, by paramedics, the military, law enforcement officers, disaster managers and many other professionals where there is a potentially high risk.

Whether your final outcome is a physical object or a mental state, you can still go "all out" for an outstanding result.

Remember, an outstanding result is where the difference between what you made or achieved or arrived at and what you planned at the start is zero and outstanding results mean effective measuring and management "on the run."

Sometimes a super-outstanding result happens. This is when your final outcome exceeds your original expectations. (Remember your surprise invitation back-stage at the rock concert in Chapter 5.) It's often when the power of your Me processor was not factored in as you viewed your initial, mental objective from a super-positive, Me-processor vantage point.

Outstanding results happen when you have an unshakable belief in the "Why" of your decision and when you have an unflinching commitment to the "What" of your decision, one that is fuelled by an undying, burning passion to make it happen. Outstanding results happen when you have a physical system poised to deliver vital, physical energy the instant it's needed and when you are viewing the world from your super-positive, Me Energy, viewing platform.

An outstanding result means an outstanding springboard for your next decision.

That truly is a formula for success.

And coming up right now - Your cool summary for success

CH 11 FOR THE DOT POINTERS

Staying on Track with Right Measurement

- **Right measurement applies to self-monitoring and self-correction as you work physically and mentally towards your final outcome.**

- Right measurement can become a powerful and useful, unconscious habit with commitment and regular practice.

- Right Outcome + Right Measurement = Right Result.

- The two "musts" for clarity in your initial mental outcome are: Identifying the <u>feeling</u> you want from the outcome of your decision and creating a detailed, mental check-list of <u>how your outcome will appear</u> when it becomes a reality.

- Primary measurement is measuring your final outcome against your initial mental idea to give you your primary result.

- Secondary measurement is measuring "on the run" as you execute the "How" part of your initial mental objective.

- Secondary measurement applies to the performance of each of your mental energy processors for the duration of your project.

- Clear and precise detailing of every important component of your initial mental objective is necessary for your mental energy processors to perform efficiently.

- Completing each stage of your project represents a mini-result.

- When a mini-result goes "pear-shaped" you will have to adjust and modify your next step and possibly the remainder of the "how-to" plan.

- **An outstanding result is when the difference between your final outcome and your initial mental outcome is zero.**

- **A super-outstanding result happens when your final outcome exceeds your initial mental expectation.**

CHAPTER 12

TEN RULES FOR MAKING THE RIGHT DECISION EVERY TIME

CHAPTER 12

TEN RULES FOR MAKING THE RIGHT DECISION EVERY TIME

RULE NO. 1: Know Thy Target

Write down, record, draw or paint or build a model of exactly what it is you want, what you're looking for, where you want to go and what you want to happen.

Scratch it in stone or on a brick. Write it in lip stick on your dressing room mirror. Describe in detail <u>exactly</u> what you want.

Do it!

It's that important!

That clear description must be there, up front in your mind's eye from the very start!

Get a picture of how life will be for you when you get what you want or find what you're looking for, arrive at the place where you want to go or feel what you want to feel.

Build the scene up. Make it big in your mind, close and even coloured if you want. "Ramp up" the feeling of what it will be like for you.

Wrap some great emotions around it.

Make it look and feel and sound terrific so that your subconscious keeps it right at the very top of its memory pile.

Remember your RAS (Reticular Activating System) is the lookout in your brain that scans the world for whatever's on top of your subconscious and conscious memory lists and it will wave fluorescent tags or prod you whenever it spots what you're after. It is the signpost that leads you to your objective. Your RAS will even send up an alert when something associated with what you want shows up. Remember the new car you bought that "everyone else" seemed to be driving or the new dress that "everyone else" seemed to be wearing as soon as you bought it. Great emotional wrapping makes you notice what's important in reaching your target, so get your Feelings processor working on the wrappings of what you're aiming for.

There's just a chance though, that what you want is the removal or elimination from your life of something (or even someone). If this is the case, getting what you want may cause some unacceptable damage or injury to whatever or whoever it is in your removal "sights."

Other people don't need to be hurt.

A better question needs to be asked:

"Why do I want that thing or that person out of my life?"

An even better question is: "What's not happening in my life right now that's creating my aversion to that person or thing?"

It's an even better question because the answer is inside <u>your</u> mind space. The object is just an object and the person just a person. They are simply perceived events ... events in your life, registered and labelled with meanings you gave them and which got wrapped in the layers of emotion you happened to be experiencing at the time. The solution to your elimination dilemma is to either change the meaning of the event in your memory or change the emotional wrapping around the memory, or both.

Your target in this case, is to fix that part of you that's not working for you at the time.

Ask yourself these two clinching questions: "What new meaning can I give this event or this thing or this person causing me grief that will make it more useful to me?"

"In what new emotion can I wrap its memory that makes it more empowering for me?"

"What new feeling will work <u>for</u> me and not against me?"

Remember, you are creating <u>your</u> world as you view it from one or more of your Me Energy processor vantage points. Changing your vantage point will change your world. Asking these simple questions automatically chooses the more useful, more empowering and right vantage point from which to view the world you have decided to change.

The old adage holds true, "If you want to change your world, you must change yourself."

So, if you did have a thing or person in your elimination sights, get it absolutely crystal clear in your mind what it is that's not happening in your life that's creating the conflict. Then write it, draw it, paint it, model it in the physical.

Target clarity is target power!

RULE NO. 2: Focus on Thy Target

Knowing your target is just that, some knowledge, some relevant pieces of information about the "something" you can't yet experience that you want included in your life.

Focusing on your objective i.e. your desired outcome, requires your Mental Energy processors to be operating at peak efficiency and in sync with each other.

A clean and efficient Critical Space in which they can operate efficiently and in sync is a must for ongoing, laser focus on your objective.

Laser focus means a keen awareness of your target and every one of its components for the duration of your journey to it.

Focus is of particular importance in the action or execution stage of your decision as it is here that the "derailers" and distracters are most likely to show up.

"There's too much going on around me. I can't concentrate on what I'm doing."

"We seem to be going backwards and not forwards. We'll never get there."

"I've been on this project for ever and more problems keep coming up. My target seems to be getting further and further away. I'm never going to make it."

Constant focus on your outcome minimizes these diversions and blocks and makes them less significant in your mind space. They become smaller and are more easily moved out of the way or stepped over or stepped around.

Constant focus on what you're aiming for keeps your target in view all the time.

RULE NO. 3: Own Thy Target

"Thy" target means "your" target and no-one else's. Others may want the same as you and may hit their target as you do however, they are not you. They will still be "them" and you will still be "you."

Remember there's one and only one of "you" ... a unique "you" that's wired as "you" and comes from that unique source of "you" intelligence. **Your target is a forwards extension of you.** You see it from where you are. No-one else can be in exactly the same spot physically or mentally as you. Even half a millimetre one way or the other is not the same. Close, yes however, not the same. You and your target are uniquely connected in this universe.

Owning your target means taking responsibility for it every step of the way and also when you reach it. You created it. You achieved it. You own it!

RULE NO. 4:   Commit to Thy Target Unflinchingly

As you chose your target in Rule No. 1, so too do you choose how to get there.

You will "hatch" a plan or come up with a strategy to make the journey. It could even be a "mud map" in your mind or more visibly on some paper or smart screen or coffee shop napkin.

Committing to your target up front means **an unflinching intent to get there no matter what.** It's the "getting-back-in-the-saddle" bit when you "fall off the horse" and the "taking-it-on-the-chin" bit when the world seems a little unfair and the "suck-it-up-princess-and-get-on-with-your-life" rule when things don't go your way.

Unflinching commitment is the powerhouse of success.

RULE NO. 5:   Know What's After Thy Target

Many a strong and stalwart human being has known and seen and owned and committed to and reached their golden summit ... won the lottery, raised a terrific family, built their dream home, acquired the Jag or jet or luxury yacht or million dollars then, bemused, surprised and sometimes even panicky ask, "What do I do now? What's next? Where to from here? It's not what I thought it would be. It's all suddenly a bit boring ... depressing even."

Arriving at your goal can be an anti-climax, a let-down and a frustrating scary void. **Knowing what's after your success keeps your life heading forwards and upwards.**

Even when the lucky break hurls the lucky gambler into instant six-figure riches, the outcome is not always good.

Figures show that many million-dollar lottery wins are lost because the lucky winner had no clarity about what came next. The dollars seemed to just leak away and the downward spiralling winner arrived back at where they were before the win ... sometimes even further behind than that.

Dollars, depression or other demoralizing downers and unplanned, severely "pear-shaped" outcomes like these are not nice, so it's best to cover those bases up front and know what comes after the win.

RULE NO. 6: Make the Journey to Thy Target

After the "Ready" and "Get set" comes the "Go!" ... the report of your mental starter's gun that signals action, the part of that wonderful and incredibly powerful I-Will processor that launches you into action (or sometimes inaction). **A target will only be reached if the first step towards it is taken.** Your I-Will processor is the star of that journey and quest. Not only does it launch you into the race or the meaningful walk or the slow and calculated manoeuver around yet another obstacle, it is also the force that "stares down" the unanticipated predicament, takes on the curve balls or hoists you back into the saddle after you fall. It has, as you now well know, the undying and magnificently engineered support of your four other mental processors: Chunks and Bits, Feelings, Physical Energy and your Me Energy. Know and believe that they are there, constantly working in your mental workshop or dressing room, moving mental energy around, in and out of your subconscious, managing and overseeing the doorway between your thoughts and your actions, driving your journey to that target, running your race and creating the magnificent stuff of your magnificent life.

RULE NO. 7: Enjoy Thy Target

So, it's happened!

You've arrived!

You're out of debt!

Your first book is published!

Your first show on the big stage was a hit!

Your biggest construction job ever has been signed off!

You got a distinction for the whole course, not just one subject!

Yay! Fantastic! Applause! Outstanding! Pat on the back. Pat on the back! Pat on the back!

Well done you!

Pile some great, positive emotion on that event. Wrap it in high-amplitude celebration and congratulations on a job outstandingly done. Decorate the emotional storage wrapper for instant recall so that you can relive a great memory further down the track and use it to spring into the next great decision. Remember, events wrapped in quality emotions are great tools for right decision making. **Positively wrapped memories build great results and make the decision journey that much easier and more enjoyable.**

RULE NO. 8: Appreciate Thy Target

Now that you've known and seen, owned and committed to and known what's after, made the journey to and enjoyed thy target, please do one more thing for yourself and the brand new bit of world you've just created for yourself. It's very important.

Please do **accept and appreciate being at the finish line,** in that new place of success you've just created for yourself. Part of that new place came from support and help along the way, from the shoulders you leaned on, "ice-breakers" that cleared your way, the healers who tended your wounds and pain-relievers who soothed your troubled brow. Some you asked for and some came freely as energy willingly volunteered and time gladly given. Some of those shoulders and ice breakers and healers you may never, ever know. Thank them all and appreciate them and their rightful place in the new you.

RULE NO. 9: Use Thy Target as a Springboard to the Next One

Now, does it all end there with celebration and thanks, applause and gratitude?

Certainly not. Remember rule number 5: "Know what's after thy target."

Whether you like it or not, you just made that recent great success and accomplishment into something special and something important and vital to your well-being.

Because you chose to scan ahead a little earlier on and dared to look beyond that target, you have turned that accomplishment into a significant, stand-out, stepping-stone event in your memory store. What's more, you will easily remember it and will likely remember it for the rest of your time on this planet, having poured so much of your great emotional energy into it. It's an event that's been registered and stored in your memory banks by your very own selective conscious effort. It's been put there by "you," consciously and deliberately. You even controlled the quality and quantity of emotional storage wrapping.

So with all you've learned from the "knocks" and "curve balls," the on-the-run corrections and the appreciation and congratulations, you now have a solid platform and vantage point from which to know and get clarity on your next objective. You had a preview in rule 5: "Know What's After Your Target." In fact, you set it up and can now, with the confidence and expertise and unstoppable driving energy of an accomplished "target reacher" and decision maker, take on the next decision, and the next ... and the next ... and the next!

RULE NO. 10: Go to Rule No. 1

Now for the Decision Maker's Golden Rule Check List.

CH 12 FOR THE DOT POINTERS

The 10 Rules for Making the Right Decision every Time

Rule No. 1   **Know Thy Target**.

Rule No. 2   **Focus on Thy Target.**

Rule No. 3   **Own Thy Target.**

Rule No. 4   **Commit to Thy Target Unflinchingly.**

Rule No. 5   **Know What's After Thy Target.**

Rule No. 6   **Make the Journey to Thy Target.**

Rule No. 7   **Enjoy Thy Target.**

Rule No. 8   Appreciate Thy Target.

Rule No. 9   Use Thy Target as a Springboard to the Next One.

Rule No. 10   Go to Rule No. 1.

CHAPTER 13

YOUR ULTIMATE DECISION

CHAPTER 13

YOUR ULTIMATE DECISION

So, now you have travelled through the pages of this work, a work dedicated to right decision making through "models," "processors," "vantage points," examples, questions, dot points and much more.

Congratulations for powering forwards through the interesting bits and "hanging in there" through those slices of text that may not have appealed at the time.

You are here now and about to read the last page and put this book down ... well maybe.

Before you do though, it's worth checking on one last question that may have been bugging you from the start. It's a question, which, should we choose to ignore it, may well be sweeping a potential and very awkward "elephant in the room," under the carpet. It's a question that may have leapt out at you from the moment you set eyes on the very front cover of the book.

So let's do one more final exercise. Let's identify the "elephant" using a little self-monitoring and ask this "elephant" question:

"The title of this book, splashed across the front page is, *"Decisions, Decisions! How to make the Right One Every Time,"* so how come there is no mention anywhere throughout the text of a "wrong" decision?"

Surely, if there are "right" decisions, there must also be "wrong" decisions?

Permit me to offer a response.

When engaging the E.C.R.O.M. Model, there can never be a "wrong" decision.

"*Decisions, Decisions*" is about decision <u>ownership</u>. Owning your decisions eliminates "wrongness" and replaces it with <u>committed measurement</u> i.e. measuring the outcome you got against the outcome you wanted from the start.

"Wrongness" is simply a "not-so-crash-hot" result ... a "wider-than-anticipated" gap between your initial mental objective and what actually happened. **Committed measurement is active learning from the decision-making experience.**

Neither do other people make "wrong" decisions. You are not them. You cannot occupy the exact same mental or physical space that they do. They are unique, as are you.

Should what others do or think <u>appear</u> to be "wrong," remember, other people's actions and thoughts represent events in your world, events that have been registered in your Critical Space.

Any "wrongness" is "meaning" you have assigned through applying your values, your beliefs, rules and unconscious habits of thought and deed.

Your meanings make your world.

Meanings are everything.

Change the meaning of what others do or think and you change your world.

Other people are simply part of your world, the world that you created or "scripted" by unconsciously channelling information into your conscious and subconscious memory banks.

There are no "wrong" decisions, just things people do.

The "elephant" and the "wrong" decision are merely mental phantoms, created through life-conditioning and habits.

So hopefully, with this "elephant" now peacefully at rest, one final and critical decision needs to be made before you cross the finish line.

And that decision right now is ...

How will you decide to use this book?

Will you flip back to a chapter or two and read them again to get some clarity because "something" pressed a button in your psyche and inspired you?

Will you put the book on the shelf alongside all the others you have read and tick the "read-it" box with no further action required?

Will you pick up the phone and call that person you know would want to read this book because you know it's exactly what they're looking for right now?

Will you set the book down, sit back for a while, ponder the read and contemplate your next move?

Whatever you choose to do with the book, rest assured, it's not the book that matters, it is what you choose to do with the <u>meanings</u> you created from the words set out on each page.

Ultimately, it is how you choose to harness the emotional energy stored up in your mind and body right now that matters.

Will you be harnessing "Wow!" energy or "what-next?" energy or "satisfaction" energy or will you be hungering for more of the same?

Whatever the energy, whatever the emotion, that energy will be the fuel that drives your very next decision to either sit tight and ponder or to step up with your brand new, decision making kit and make a difference in your life and in the lives of those around you.

My hope is for the latter.

May your every decision from this point forwards be a right decision and an absolute winner.

Surprise, surprise! No dot points needed.

ABOUT THE AUTHOR

STEVE COLEMAN

Author, Educator, Entrepreneur, Pilot & Outdoorsman

Steve is an author, educator, father and outdoorsman.

While a Cadet Under Officer in the North Queensland Squadron Air Training Corps, Steve made his first solo flight at the age of 18. After being awarded a teaching scholarship, he attended James Cook University and University of New England.

Steve's training helped him enjoy 18 years as the Outdoor Education Coordinator for Townsville Grammar School. When his entrepreneurial spirit inspired him, he resigned from full-time employment and started his own education company. He now contracts to numerous schools, colleges, businesses, youth and sporting organisations.

He also enjoys the outdoors. Since 1985, Steve has led more than 30,000 children and young adults on excursions, expeditions and camping trips. Additionally, he is an avid supporter of skydiving, mountaineering and marathon running.

Steve has worked with a wide variety of companies, schools, and organisations. The list includes several Queensland high schools, most of the private secondary schools in Townsville and hinterland, several local sports clubs, Youth Services of Queensland, several Army cadet units and Queensland Guides and Scouts.

His professional associations include the International Yoga Teachers Association, Queensland College of Teachers, Queensland Writers' Centre, Townsville Writers and Publishers' Centre and Queensland Outdoor Recreation Federation. He is also a Registered Consultant with Kolbe Corporation in Phoenix, Arizona, USA.

Steve has lived, travelled and worked throughout New Zealand, Papua New Guinea, USA, Canada, Singapore, UK, Malaysia and the Cook Islands.

Steve Coleman is the author of "Decisions, Decisions!" and four children's books; "The Bee's Knees," "The Ant's Pants," "Naree the Fire Lady" and "Jodi and The Turtle." He lives in Queensland, Australia.

RECOMMENDED RESOURCES

KOLBE CORP

www.kolbe.com

info@kolbe.com

2355 E Camelback Rd

Suite 610 Phoenix,
AZ 85016 USA

(602) 840-9770
(800) 642-2822

International Yoga Teacher's Association (IYTA)

Enquiries:
info@iyta.org.au

Teacher Training:
teachertraining@iyta.org.au

Pre & Post Natal Teacher Training:
prenatal@iyta.org.au

Post Graduate Teacher Training:
postgrad@iyta.org.au

p: 1800 449 195

IYTA GPO Box 57, Sydney NSW 2001

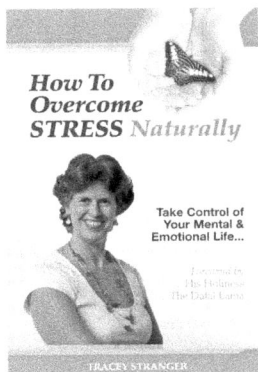

Tracey Stranger

Scientist (Microbiologist), Strategic Marketer,

Time Line Therapy Trainer,

NLP Master Trainer & Hypnotherapist,

Taoist Self Healing exercises & Stillness Meditation,

Soul Centred Astrologer, Ancient Wisdom Teachings

Life Mastery workshops,

One Minute Meditation App,

Entrepreneur and Author

Read more at
www.HowToOvercomeStressNaturally.com

Contact: inspire@traceystranger.com

Mobile: 0409 879 271

Kevin Lloyd-Thomas

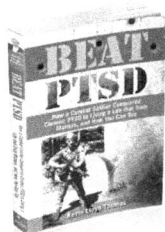

(F) www.facebook.com/
     networkforveteran

(w) www.networkfor
     veteransuccess.com

GLOSSARY OF TERMS, COLLOQUIALISMS AND SLANG

Foreword

Human demography

Study of population statistics in human communities

Introduction

Brewing

In the making.

Chapter 1

Acronym

A word formed from the initial letters of other words.

Armageddon

The place where the final great battle will be fought between the forces of good and evil.

Autonomic nervous system

The part of the nervous system that controls the automatic function of glands, blood vessels, heart and smooth muscles.

Critical Space

That part of the mind where incoming data is processed before a corresponding response or reaction occurs i.e. between stimulus and response.

E.C.R.O.M. Solution

The set of strategies that use the E.C.R.O.M. Model of decision making to live a healthier mental, physical and spiritual life.

Event

A change in one's physical environment either detected or undetected by the senses or a change in mental state of which one may or may not be aware.

Event registering

Changes in one's physical or mental environment that are deemed significant enough by the relevant parts of the brain for further processing.

Internal event loop

A conscious or unconscious change in one's mental environment e.g. a new idea based on a memory.

Keeping heads above water

Staying alive, surviving, keeping a project viable.

Making ends meet

Just keeping up with demand, usually financially.

Phagocyte

A cell that engulfs and destroys foreign particles, bacteria and harmful cells, found mostly in blood and lymphatic tissue.

Post Traumatic Stress Disorder (PTSD)

A mental disorder following a traumatic event outside normal experience.

Rocks up

Arrives.

Runs rough

The result when compression of fuel in an internal combustion engine is out of time with the electrical sparking inside the combustion chamber. An engine running rough is not at its most powerful.

Tad

A little or small amount.

Tizz

Frantic and ineffective state of activity.

Yogini

A female yoga practitioner.

Chapter 2

Adrenaline

A body chemical (hormone) that prepares the body for dealing with threat of harm or stress.

Affective system

Mental system relating to feelings.

Awareness vantage point

The energy state that creates one's particular view of the world.

Below par

Not up to the desired or expected standard.

Big Bang (the)

The theorised origin of the universe with a single explosion of super-dense matter.

Bomb-proof

Very strong. Can withstand extreme shock, impact or rigorous scrutiny.

Caught between a rock and a hard place

When both escape routes from a difficult situation are themselves very dangerous or appear impossible.

Chunks and Bits processor

That part of the mind that organises finite pieces of information in a logical way. The cognitive part of the mind.

Close shave

A near miss.

Cognitive

Intellectual. Thinking logically.

Conation

The part of mental activity that relates to striving. Wilfully doing (or not doing). Making an effort.

Conative energy

The mental energy of maintaining effort or endeavour.

Deoxyribonucleic acid (DNA)

A large molecule found in the nucleus of cells and viruses responsible for passing on characteristics of the parents to offspring.

Death zone

Zone on a mountain above 8,000 metres (26,000 feet approx.) where there is not enough oxygen for humans to breathe easily.

Electroencephalogram (EEG)

The graphic record from a device that measures the electrical activity of the brain.

Empirical science

Science based on experimentation.

Fast-track

Speed up the process.

Full tilt

Operating at maximum power or with maximum effort.

Full swing

All systems in an operation or endeavour are completely under way.

Glitches

Minor obstacles or set-backs.

Graveyard shift

In the dead of night, usually between 2 and 4 AM.

Feelings processor

The part of the mind that deals with feelings (emotions) and values. The affective part of the mind.

Gobsmacked

Astounded and surprised, sometimes expressed in open-mouthed, silent amazement.

Hang in there

Stay focussed and keep applying your best effort. (because) "You are almost there."

Hard wired

Permanently attached or very strongly embedded.

Hypothermia

A physical and mental condition where body temperature is significantly below normal [less than 35.0 °C (95.0 °F)] Normal body temperature is 36.5–37.5 °C (97.7–99.5 °F)

Intelligence quotient (IQ)

The comparison of mental age against chronological age as decided by specially designed tests.

I Will processor

The part of the mind that deals with wilfulness, intent and the impulse to do (or not do) something.

Logic

Principles of reasoning applied to any branch of knowledge or study.

Me Energy processing platform

The energy state that creates one's particular view of the world.

Me Energy processor

The part of the mind that deals with healing and different states of awareness.

Out of sync.

Unsynchronised. Timing of events that normally work together is out. Not co-ordinated.

Physical Energy processor

That part of the mind that deals with physical movement and maintenance of the body.

Psychomotor

Relating to voluntary movement.

Result

The difference between the desired outcome and the outcome that actually occurs.

Run like the proverbial

Run fast. Run like a hare.

Run the race

Carry out a mission. Get to an objective.

Scientific method

A method of solving a problem or answering a question by initially forming an hypothesis followed by relevant experimentation and then evaluation of the experimental result.

Spin-Off

Side effect.

Subconscious

Mental activity of which we are not aware.

Trump card

Single important advantage.

Turfing out

Throwing away. Discarding.

Wacky

Out of the ordinary. Eccentric.

Wiped off the map

Totally destroyed or removed.

Chapter 3

Behaviourism

The study of human behaviour in terms of human response to environmental stimuli.

Big time

Fully occupying the space. Fully extended. Total commitment.

Brought to heel

Bring back into control or manageable state.

Cornice

Wind-formed over-hang on the top of a mountain high point.

Dodged the death bullet

Had a narrow escape from death.

Electro-chemistry

System where chemical activity produces electricity and vice versa.

Gang up

Form a group that opposes another person or group.

Hard yards

Hard work.

Have a hand in

Be a part of.

Hissy fit

Temper tantrum.

Internal thought loops

The same as internal event loops where a thought triggers another thought.

In the pipeline

Already deployed or engaged.

Leave (you) in the lurch

Put (you) in an uncomfortable or helpless position.

Lie-in

Not get out of bed (because it's comfortable).

Max out

Extend to maximum effect.

Par for the course

A normal expectation for (that) activity.

Put in some yards

Put in time and effort.

Rain check

To postpone accepting an invitation.

Reaction

Usually unconscious action resulting from either physical or mental stimulus.

Reflex arc

Movement of nervous impulse that produces an unintended, (normally) physical movement.

Response

Reasoned or calculated, conscious action resulting from a physical or mental stimulus.

Rub salt into the wound

To make an emotional injury worse.

Shape up

Get organised and ready for the task.

Sour grapes

Putting down or not accepting an idea simply because it's not liked.

Stimulus-response psychology

Same as behaviourism: The study of human behaviour in terms of human response to environmental stimuli.

Wash its hands of

Not have anything to do with. Choosing to not be responsible for an action or idea.

Chapter 4

A bit slack

A bit lazy.

Down in the dumps

Temporarily depressed, sad or unhappy.

Execution

The action part of the decision process occurring between the initial idea of what is desired and the actual outcome that really happens.

Take on the chin

Accept a hurt without judgment.

Outcome

The mental idea of what is wanted initially or the end product of a decision i.e. what actually happened.

Chapter 5

Animalia

The animal kingdom.

In sync.

Synchronised. Working together harmoniously.

In the black

In profit.

IPod

A portable music player developed by Apple Computers.

Fight or flight

Instinctive response to a threat, which readies one either to resist forcibly or to run away.

Fly in the ointment

A flaw that greatly reduces the value or enjoyment of something.

Homeostasis

Balance within living creatures between body functions and the chemicals that control them.

Hypothalamus

Part of the middle brain concerned with emotional responses and homeostasis.

Measurement

Comparing the final outcome of a decision i.e. what actually happened, with the outcome that was initially desired.

Neolithic

Latter part of the Stone Age.

New age

Social revolution based on non-traditional views about health, medicine and the environment.

Nitty-gritty

The basic essentials of an issue.

Off the mark

Off target.

<u>Transition</u>

Bucket list

List of things one wants to do or achieve.

Cosmic (Universal) Intelligence

Positive energy of creation.

Curve balls

Unexpected events that can potentially compromise the success of a project.

Ruminate

Ponder. Meaningfully and quietly consider.

Universal field of intelligence

The unobservable background to all that happens in the universe.

Take on board

Accept and include as a working part (of a project or team).

Chapter 6

Carrier decision

A decision used as an excuse to fulfil a strong desire or to continue a habit which can be either empowering or disempowering.

Constructive self-reflection

Positively thinking back over events in order to improve performance in the future.

Ginormous

Unbelievably big.

Letting the side down

Wilfully not living up to expectations or standards.

Nail (this)

Conclusively succeed (in doing this).

Neanderthals

A "race" of humans believed to be ancestors of modern man that inhabited Europe 40,000 to 10,000 years ago.

(Go) pear-shaped

Go wrong. Break down. Success is compromised.

Out of the blue

Totally unexpected.

Chapter 7

Back in the game

Returned to active engagement in the project.

Has it in for (me)

Picking on (me). Singling (me) out based on unfair reasoning.

Out of whack

Out of alignment. Off course.

Reticular Activating System (RAS)

A powerful processing part of the lower brain that processes nervous impulses entering the brain from below. It also filters out repetitive, familiar or weak signals from the incoming sensory impulses.

Chapter 8

State of play

Up to date information about what's happening.

8.1

Yardstick

Reference point against which other information can be compared.

Laws of manifestation

The natural laws that govern the bringing of potential or possibility into reality.

8.2

Off beat

Not synchronised, out of tune.

Sweet spot

Point of impact (on a bat, tennis racquet, baseball bat etc.) that consistently delivers great results.

Going swimmingly

Going magnificently.

Dropped off the radar

Disappeared from view.

Chapter 9

Out of the blue

Totally unexpected.

Chapter 10

Chapter 11

All out

Complete and convincing.

On the run

As the action unfolds.

Chapter 12

Ice Breaker

A person who prepares ahead for an action to be carried out by themselves or someone else.

On the run

Escaped or hiding from pursuit.

Fall off the horse

Have an accident.

Paramedic

Specialist in giving assistance of a medical nature e.g. ambulance officer.

Ramp up

Intensify.

Chapter 13

High amplitude

Loud. A large distance between wave crests and troughs.

Ice (breaking the)

Breaking the initial tension in a group when they meet for the first time.

Jag.

Jaguar – a brand of luxury car.

Mud map

A roughly drawn map, not always to scale.

Taking it on the chin

Accepting an emotional or physical injury with grace or dignity and then moving on.

The elephant in the room

A troublesome issue that everyone chooses to ignore however, it is one of which everyone is aware.

RECOMMENDED READING & REFERENCES

The Top 5

Deepak Chopra — "Ageless Body, Timeless Mind. A Practical Alternative to Growing Old"
Pub. Harmony Books 1993.
(w) www.deepakchopra.com

Kathy Kolbe — "Conative Connection. Acting on Instinct"
Pub. Kathy Kolbe 1990 – 1997.
(w) www.kolbe.com

Stephen R Covey — "The 7 Habits of Highly Effective People. Powerful Lessons in Personal Change"
Pub. Free Press. A division of Simon and Schuster.1989, 2004.
(w) www.stephencovey.com/7habits/7habits.php

Anthony Robbins — "Awaken The Giant Within. How to take control of your mental, emotional, physical and financial destiny"
Pub. Simon and Schuster Ltd. 1992.
(w) www.tonyrobbins.com

Sir Ken Robinson — "The Element. How Finding Your Passion Changes Everything"
Pub. Allen Lane 2009
(w) www.ted.com/speakers/sir_ken_robinson

...And more

Stephen R Covey	"The 8th Habit. From Effectiveness to Greatness" Pub. Free Press. A division of Simon and Schuster.1989, 2004.
Malcolm Gladwell	"The Tipping Point. How Little Things Can Make a Big Difference" Pub. Back Bay Books/Little Brown and Company. Hachette Book Group.
Elaine N. Marieb	"Human Anatomy and Physiology" Pub. The Benjamin/Cummings Publishing Company, Inc. 1989.
Zoe-Anne Fields	"Transformations. A Guided Journal" Pub. Vivid Publishing 2015.
Stephen W. Hawking	"A Brief History of Time. From The Big Bang To Black Holes" Pub. Bantam Press 1991.
Joe Simpson	"Touching The Void" Pub. Vintage 2004.
Phillip Day	"The ABC'S Of Disease" Pub. Credence Publications 2003. "the mind game" Pub. Credence Publications 2002.
Helen Irlen	"Reading by the Colours. Overcoming Dyslexia and Other Reading Disabilities Through the Irlen Method" Pub. The Berkley Publishing Group 1991, 2005.
Kathy Kolbe	"Pure Instinct. The M.O. of High Performance People and Teams" Pub. Monumentus Press 1993 – 2004.

Deepak Chopra	"The Seven Spiritual Laws of Success. A Pocketbook Guide To Fulfilling Your Dreams" Pub. Amber-Allen Publishing Inc. 1994, 2007.
W.E. Bowman	"The Ascent of Rum Doodle" Pub. Pimlico 2001.
Brian Tracy	"Eat That Frog. 21 Great Ways to Stop Procrastinating and Get More Done in Less Time" Pub. Berrett-Koehler Publishers, Inc. 2001, 2002.
Edward De Bono	"Six Thinking Hats" Pub. Penguin Books 1985 1999
Paramahansa Yogananda	"Autobiography of a Yogi" Pub. Self-Realisation Fellowship 2007.
Sri Nisargadatta Maharaj	"I Am That" Pub. Acorn Press 1988.
Carlos Castaneda	"The Teachings of Don Juan" Pub. University of California Press 1968; Penguin Books 1970-1986. "A Separate Reality" Pub. Washington Square Press 1991. "Journey to Ixtlan" Pub. Penguin Books and Bodley Head 1972-1974. "Tales of Power" Pub. Penguin Books 1974-1978. "The Second Ring of Power" Pub. Penguin Books 1977-1979. "The Eagle's Gift" Pub. Penguin Books 1981-1982. "The Fire from Within" Pub. Black Swan 1984-1985. "The Art of Dreaming" Pub. Harper Collins 1994.

Carl Zimmer	"Secrets of the Brain" Article. National Geographic Magazine Feb. 2014 Vol. 225. No. 2. Pub. National Geographic Society 2014.
Jonathon Foley	"A Five-step Plan to Feed the Planet" Article. National Geographic Magazine. May 2014 Vol.225. No. 5. Pub. National Geographic Society 2014.
David Quammen	"A Hundred Years Ago" Article. National Geographic Magazine. Jan. 2016 Vol. 229. No 1. Pub. National Geographic Society 2016.
Prof. Michael A. Roberto	"The Art of Critical Decision Making. Vol 1 of 2" The Great Courses. 12 Lectures (CD) Course No 5932 2009 The Teaching Company.
John Thie DC and Matthew Thie, Ed	"Touch for Health. A Practical Guide to Natural Health With Acupressure Touch" Pub. DeVorss & Company 2005.
Paul Warren (With Jeff Apton)	"The Fighter. The Extraordinary True Story of How a Muay Thai Champion Survived Hell on the Frontline in Afghanistan" Pub. Allen Unwin 2015.
Dr Ross Walker	"Lose Weight, Gain Energy & Live Longer by Optimising Your Cell Health with The Cell Factor" Pub. Pan McMillan Australia Pty. Ltd. 2002 – 2006

Gary Chapman

"The Five Love Languages. How to Express
Heartfelt Commitment to Your Mate"
Pub. Strand Publishing 2000 – 2009

Tracey Stranger

"How to Overcome Stress Naturally. Take
Control of Your Mental and Emotional Life"
F/W HH The 14th Dalai Lama.
Pub. Global Publishing Group March 2012)

OTHER REFERENCES

Aristotle

(384 – 322 BC) was a Greek philosopher and scientist whose writings cover many subjects including the first comprehensive system of Western philosophy. (Ch. 3)

(René) Descartes

16-17th Century French philosopher, mathematician and scientist on whose work modern philosophy is mostly based. (Ch. 3)

(John) Locke

17th Century English philosopher, physician and influential thinker leading up to the 18th Century, European "Age of Enlightenment." (Ch. 3)

Patanjali

The yogi master believed to be responsible for assembling the "Yoga Sutra" which is the guidebook of classical or raja (royal) yoga and written at least 1,700 years ago.

Benjamin Bloom

(1913 – 1999) was an American educational psychologist who made contributions to classifying the cognitive aspects of the mind. (Ch. 8)

Jean Piaget

(1896 – 1980) was a Swiss psychologist and philosopher known for his studies of knowledge and justified belief in the education of children. He also contributed new ideas to the understanding of human cognitive development. (Ch. 8)

Sigmund Freud

(1856 – 1939) was an Austrian neurologist who pioneered a clinical method for treating mental illness through dialogue between a patient and a trained specialist (psychoanalyst). (Ch. 8)

Dr. Clare W. Graves Ph D.

(1914 – 1986) was a visionary thinker who began laying the groundwork for the theory behind the SPIRAL DYNAMICS®. He was a specialist in theories of personality and their applications all the while addressing the question of which theory most accurately depicted the development of human nature.

www.ingramcontent.com/pod-product-compliance
Lightning Source LLC
Chambersburg PA
CBHW060017100426
42740CB00010B/1506